The $1.98 Cookbook

How to Eat Like A Gourmet And Save $6,000—Or More—A Year

Other Books by Carl Japikse:

The Hour Glass
The Biggest Tax Cheat in America is the I.R.S.
Poems of Light
The Light Within Us
Exploring the Tarot
Pigging Out in Columbus
Teeing Off in Central Ohio
A Golfer's Guide To Breaking 80

with Robert R. Leichtman, M.D.:

Active Meditation
The Art of Living
The Life of Spirit
Forces of the Zodiac
Healing Lines
Ruling Lines
Connecting Lines

as Waldo Japussy:

The Tao of Meow

The $1.98 Cookbook

How To Eat Like A Gourmet
And Save $6,000—Or More—A Year

A Cookbook by Carl Japikse

ENTHEA PRESS
Atlanta, Georgia

TABLE OF CONTENTS

Introduction — page 7

The $1.98 Budget — page 10

Sharpen Your Knives — page 19

Get Into the Kitchen! — page 23

Breakfast — page 27

Lunches & Light Suppers — page 45

Entrées — page 73

Vegetables — page 105

Desserts — page 125

Breads — page 137

Homemade Everything — page 147

The $1.98 Challenge — page 153

Index — page 159

To my mother,
Marion Japikse,
who taught me
the basics of
cooking for less

Introduction

The idea for this cookbook first popped into mind on Thanksgiving Day a number of years ago. My wife and I were watching the evening news, and they were interviewing people who "might not have as much to be thankful for" as the rest of us. One of the couples who did not feel thankful was filmed at home in their trailer with their two children. Even though the husband worked, they were feeling the pinch of just getting by on a tight budget. "I can't remember the last time we had steaks," the husband complained.

I looked at my wife and asked her, "Do you remember having steaks when you were growing up?" She said no. They ate well, but they certainly never had filet mignon. That was my experience, too.

The next night, we were watching the news again. The story was of an Asian immigrant who had arrived in this country a few years before without a penny to his name. While working at whatever jobs he could find, he ate simple meals of rice that cost him only 50 cents to a dollar a day. He saved the rest of the money he might have spent on food. After a few years, he had saved enough to open his own restaurant. It had now been open one year, and it was doing so well that he was giving money back to his regular patrons, in gratitude for their support.

The contrast between these two stories left a very strong impression. Many of the problems we face in society today are caused simply because many people do not know how to do any better. The Asian immigrant knew how to exist on next to nothing, and was therefore able to tap into the rich abundance of the

American dream. But the other fellow–and his wife–resented having to live on a modest income. As a result, they were estranged from the American dream. Even worse, they felt abandoned by society. So they were unable to be grateful for the riches they did have–a comfortable place to live, two healthy children, clothes to wear, food for the table, a car, and a TV.

As rich as our society is, these riches do not do us any good if we are unable to tap them and put them to work for ourselves. In some ways, our rapid advancements have exacerbated this problem. One hundred years ago, men and women knew how to feed themselves from their garden and from wild game; they knew how to cook on a wood stove–or even an open fire. They might have had little spending money in their pockets, but they knew how to eat well.

Today, many of us have forgotten these important lessons of life. We have been lulled into believing that cooking is a process of opening a box of Hamburger Helper™ or Stovetop Stuffing.™ As a result, we spend our food money unwisely, and then cannot understand why we cannot afford to eat better.

As a youth, I spent my junior year in high school as an exchange student living with a family in Quito, Ecuador. Although this was a middle class, prosperous family by Ecuadorian standards, they had no car and no refrigerator. The meals–and they were delicious–were cooked on a woodburning stove. The kitchen was a simple affair–a couple of cupboards, a work table, and the stove. No Corian™ counters, no can openers, and no electric knives. Cuisinart™ was not spoken there.

And yet we ate well. The live-in maid went to the neighborhood grocer each morning and bought the foods required for the day. The milkman delivered fresh milk every morning, just as it used to happen in this country. I learned that you do not need fancy equipment to fix good food–a principle that still holds true today, even though most of us have forgotten it.

And you do not need a big budget. I decided to investigate the true story behind the cost of eating in America today. I started paying attention to the cost of food–and the cost of the recipes I enjoy fixing. I was amazed by what I found.

First, it is possible to eat a wholesome, well-prepared dinner for less than $1.98 a person–not just occasionally, but every night of the week.

Second, it is possible to eat a good hearty breakfast and a solid lunch for a combined cost of $1.98 a person.

Together, that means the average adult can eat well for less than $4 a day–about $1500 a year.

But that's not all. If it suits your taste, you can eat like a gourmet for these small sums of money–or less.

You can even have steak! I will show you how it can be done.

Actually, taking the book as a whole, the average cost per day of my recipes is well under $3–far less than the amount the government provides in food stamps to people with no income.

But if I had to, I could eat well and prosper on a total food budget of $1.98 a day. That's for breakfast, lunch, and dinner all put together–$700 a year, or $600 less than the amount given food stamp recipients. I will show you how it can be done in the last chapter.

Of course, you may not need to watch your budget this closely. But if you are like so many Americans–students, young adults, newlyweds, and senior citizens who must make their food budget count for as much as they can–I think you will find this book illuminating and helpful. It will show you the way to eat better, enjoy it more, and save a lot of money.

9

The $1.98 Budget

It is not at all difficult to eat like a gourmet on a bare-bones budget. Throughout the world, the heart and soul of every great cuisine are the dishes that have been developed by the peasants, the serfs, the slaves, the transient, and the poor. In the East, fried rice is a wonderful dish that costs only a few pennies to serve. In Italy, the cuisine centers on pasta. The great symbol of French cooking is French bread–the cheapest form of bread known to mankind. Shish kabobs are the invention of Middle Eastern bandits. Tacos and burritos are the inspiration of the Aztecs. Most potato dishes were invented by folks who couldn't afford to put meat on the table.

The art of eating well on a limited budget is to accept the financial restriction without begrudging it. If you feed your family nothing but tuna casseroles and macaroni and cheese, it is not because you cannot afford anything better. It is because you are not managing your food dollars wisely.

Most people on a tight budget start relying on "fillers" and "extenders" to compensate. This sends an instant message to everyone eating the meal: "we're having to cut corners again." And it probably tastes like it, too.

The recipes in this book do not use fillers or extenders in order to save money. They use ingredients that have been carefully chosen to taste good, provide nutrition, and satisfy the heartiest appetite. They also happen to be inexpensive. But that can be our little secret. Your family never needs to know it. And they will certainly never guess it, if you start feeding them the dishes I have collected here.

One of my recommendations, for example, is to serve turkey more often. Many people think they are too poor to afford this traditional American Thanksgiving treat. But this is not true. Turkey is one of the great meat bargains available. It is usually possible to buy a whole turkey for as little as 69 cents a pound. Fix it with stuffing and a fresh vegetable and you will have a great Sunday dinner–for about 60 cents a person. But even more importantly, you will have great leftovers. Out of a 16 pound turkey, you should be able to get the equivalent of 24 servings. That should include sliced meat for at least three dinners, smaller slices for turkey sandwiches, turkey scraps baked as turkey tetrazzini, and turkey salad. This still leaves the carcass, which can be used to make turkey soup and turkey stock. This comes out to an average of 40 cents a serving.

In New Zealand, they would call this kind of meal a "weekend joint." It could be a pot roast, a leg of lamb, or some other meat. The idea is to buy a large amount of meat at an economical price, cook it, and then enjoy it all weekend. If you have a refrigerator or freezer, you can spread the enjoyment out for weeks or months, so it does not become boring.

At the other end of the spectrum, I have also tried to collect recipes that skillfully, artfully, and tastefully make a small portion of meat go a long way–without being obvious about it. Fried rice is a good example of this principle. You can have a delicious fried rice with shrimp, pork, or beef, yet use only two ounces of meat per serving. Or you can fix a rich dish like beef Stroganoff. By serving it as a stuffed baked potato, you can keep the meat portion down to 2 to 3 ounces.

The real key to eating like a gourmet on a starvation diet is to improve your shopping skills. We should be grateful that we live in a land of plenty, where food costs are downright inexpensive–if we know how to shop. In Russia, shoppers line up and wait for hours for the opportunity to buy meat or fish or vegetables or whatever the shop deals in. Because these items are scarce, they also end up costing quite a bit. In this country, most of us have access to half a dozen different grocery stores within a 10-minute radius of our home. Half of them are probably open 24 hours a day and will take checks or credit cards as well as cash. Because they compete with one another for your food dollar, it is usually possible to get some phenomenal deals–if you look for them.

In the last few years, wholesale clubs have sprung up all across the country–and they all feature large grocery sections where you can buy staples and produce alike. We belong to a club called Pace; in other parts of the country, they are called Price, Sam's Club, and so on. If you are willing to buy in bulk, you can often get incredible bargains at these clubs–more so on the staples and dairy products than on the produce.

If you live near a food co-op, you might want to check out its prices, too. Since co-ops are owned by their customers, they usually are good places to save money. There is no co-op near where I live on the north side of Atlanta, but there is a farmers market–a mammoth warehouse that offers fresh vegetables, fruits, meats, fish, and breads. Our market is called Harry's, and I wouldn't think of buying fruits or vegetables anywhere else. On a day when every other store is selling a head of lettuce for 97 cents, for example, Harry's may well be selling it for 59 cents. It's fresher, too.

It is not always practical for folks on a limited budget to visit half a dozen different stores, just to find the right prices. But it usually is possible to plan your shopping so that you go to a different store every time

Getting Your 2 Cents Worth:

Coffee – 1 cent a cup
Tea – 1 cent a cup
Margarine – 1 cent per tablespoon
Sugar cookies – 1 cent a cookie
Homemade vanilla extract – 1 cent a teaspoon
Homemade French bread – 1 cent a slice
Sugar – 1 cent per tablespoon
Flour – 1 cent per 1/4 cup
Oatmeal raisin cookies – 2 cents a cookie
Milk – 2 cents and ounce
Homemade wheat bread – 2 cents a slice
Peanut butter – 1 cent a serving
Corn muffin – 2 cents a piece
Dinner rolls – 2 cents a roll
Homemade English muffins – 2 cents each

you do shop. And if you do not live close to a warehouse club or a farmer's market, it may be a good idea to form a carpool with your neighbors and make the trip to the closest one at least once every two weeks.

To obtain information for this book, I priced food costs for several months at my neighborhood Kroger's, Ingles, Winn Dixie, Bruno's, A & P, and Cub. I also shopped at Pace warehouse club and at Harry's farmers market. All of the costs per serving I quote were actual prices found in at least one of these stores; none of them was based on coupons or "loss leader" come-ons requiring minimum purchases. As a result of this research, I learned several important things:

· Avoid impulse buying. Make a shopping list and stick to it as much as possible. Don't just buy something "because it looks good." For this reason, leave your children at home when you shop, if at all possible. Children are impulse buyers, and will nag you to death to get what they want. It is likewise not a good idea to shop when you are hungry or tired.

· Shop for food value, not commercial appeal. Soft drinks, for instance, are a very poor buy on a limited budget. Even if you buy your soda at a warehouse, the cheapest you can expect to buy it for is 24 cents a can. If you drink two or three cans a day, you have put a major dent into your $1.98 budget. Obviously, beer and wine are even more costly. By comparison, a cup of coffee or a cup of tea can cost as little as 1 cent to brew– if you buy the coffee or tea at a warehouse club. A cup of cocoa can cost as little as 4 cents. Sugar-free Kool Aid™ costs only 4 cents for an 8-ounce glass, including the sugar you add. (At 9 cents a glass, the pre-sugared Kool Aid™ is a wasteful purchase.)

Dramatic savings like these suggest a number of cost saving strategies. Instead of buying coffee at work or on the road, take a thermos of home brewed coffee with you. Instead of drinking a can of soda, drink a glass of iced tea or orange juice instead. In Atlanta, it is often possible to buy a half gallon of orange juice for 99 cents. That's 12 cents for an 8-ounce glass.

If you are raising kids, be sure they get at least 2 to 3 glasses of milk a day. At 12 cents for an 8-ounce glass, it's a good buy.

· Buy food, not processing or packaging. Here's a simple test you can conduct yourself. The next time you shop, take the cash register tape and check every item that costs $2 or more. Unless it is a meat or fish item, you will find that the majority of these items have been heavily processed–a TV dinner, a box of cereal, a frozen dessert, or a box of breakfast burritos. These are convenience foods, but we end up paying a dear price

Cost per serving:

Milk – 2 cents an ounce
Grits – 3 cents a serving
Butter – 3 cents a tablespoon
Cabbage – 3 cents a serving
Pumpkin – 3 cents a serving
Homemade pasta – 4 cents a serving
Rice – 4 cents a serving
Bacon – 5 cents a slice
Catsup – 5 cents an ounce
Kiwi – 6 cents per half
Large eggs – 6 cents each
Shrimp – 6 cents each
Bananas – 7 cents each
American cheese – 7 cents a slice
Canteloupe – 7 cents a slice
Fresh corn – 8 cents an ear
Carrots – 8 cents each
Potatoes – 8 cents a serving
Orange juice – 9 cents a serving
Lettuce – 9 cents a wedge
Grapefruit – 10 cents per half
Kiwi – 10 cents per half
Sausage – 10 cents an ounce
Onions – 12 cents each
Fresh asparagus – 16 cents a serving
Yams – 18 cents a serving
Frozen broccoli – 19 cents a serving
Ground beef or turkey – 25 cents a serving
Ham – 35 cents a serving
Catfish nuggets – 40 cents a serving
Turkey – 40 cents a serving
Fried chicken – 50 cents a serving

for a little bit of convenience. It is usually much cheaper to buy the raw ingredients and process them ourselves. That is, after all, what we call "cooking."

If you buy cooked shrimp ready for shrimp cocktail, for example, you may end up spending as much as $11.99 a pound. Or you could buy large green shrimp in the shell for $3.99 a pound and cook them and peel them yourself, a process that will take about 15 minutes. For 15 minutes work, you can save $8. That's $32 an hour. And you are eating shrimp, which otherwise would be too expensive for your budget.

Here are some other examples of how you can save by not buying processed and packaged foods:

You can buy toaster waffles for 12 cents a toast-sized piece. You can make a fresh waffle of the same size for 2 cents–and it will taste much better.

You can make instant mashed potatoes for 30 cents a serving–or real mashed potatoes from scratch for 15 cents a serving. You can buy a bag of frozen french fries for $1.15 a pound–or you can make your own for 15 cents a pound.

You can buy Stovetop Stuffing™ for 25 cents a serving. You can make better stuffing for 8 cents a serving.

You can buy a scrambled egg and bacon breakfast for $1.59. You can make the same breakfast yourself for 35 cents–and that includes grapefruit and coffee!

You can buy a spinach soufflé for $1.79. You can make a better one in less time than it takes to cook the frozen one for just 54 cents.

You can buy a package of flavored oatmeal for 25 cents. You can make your own for just 4 cents.

The list goes on and on. As a general rule, the more a food has been processed, the more expensive it will be. The more elaborate its packaging, the more you are paying for plastic and cardboard, not food value. You

16

are, in essence, flushing your money down the drain.

In buying bacon, for example, you can often get a better deal by buying the store's own bacon, at the meat counter, rather than a prepackaged brand name. And if you are lucky, you may be able to buy bacon "odds and ends" at the meat counter for a huge savings.

I am often able to buy a pound of smoked pork chunks for as little as 49 cents. I use these for omelets, quesadillas, fillups, ham croquettes, and popups. Why pay more for packaging you throw away?

In a few rare cases, of course, you may be able to reap savings and convenience both. Unless a vegetable is in season, it may be cheaper to buy it frozen than fresh. This is especially true of peas, lima beans, and other legumes. Corn and carrots, on the other hand, are usually cheaper fresh.

When it comes to pricey vegetables, such as asparagus, you should only buy them in season. As a rule of thumb, I would never buy asparagus unless the price was $1.99 a pound or less–and it would need to be good quality. In season, however, the price may plunge to 99 cents a pound–or even lower. Then it is a great buy. In preparing asparagus, you should always snap the stems where they crisply break in two. Save the tip end of the stalks for Chinese asparagus (page 111). Save the other ends for an asparagus soufflé (page 117). Before making the soufflé, however, cut off the last inch of the stalk–and save it for your vegetable stock. In this way you can trim the cost per serving down to 16 cents–and the vegetable stock is free!

I am not a fan of canned foods, unless there is no alternative. The nutritive level and quality of foods is highest when foods are fresh. The food level declines somewhat during the freezing process, but even more when commercially canned. Some canned foods are

17

cheaper than fresh–but you would be surprised by the ones that are not. Like tuna. If you buy it by the can, you will be paying $5.75 or higher per pound. I found fresh tuna in New York city for just $3.89 a pound.

For this reason, I view baby foods as a poor buy, too. You are paying an awful lot for a tiny jar and for food that has been highly processed. It is more sensible–and economical–to purée a small portion of whatever you are eating in a blender. It only takes about 5 seconds.

You may be able to save even more by using coupons and by taking advantage of other specials. Grocery stores will often mark down certain fruits, vegetables, and meats in order to sell them more quickly. These are not spoiled or defective items–just ones that did not sell as quickly as expected. You may even be able on occasion to pick up perfectly good filet mignon at the cost of a rump roast.

Along this line, Harry's–our farmers market–offers a crate of fresh fruits for just $3.50. You have to take what Harry gives you, of course–you don't get to make up your own crate. But this represents an enormous value to a family that can consume that much fruit. Pace likewise offers a grabbag of fruit for $3.95.

By staying alert for special offers such as these, you can make your food dollar go even further than I have indicated in this book. Remember, the $1.98 challenge is based on the regular minimum prices I have found–not on specials such as the ones I have just described or coupon purchasing. If you manage the shopping process wisely, you can unquestionably trim even more fat out of your food dollar. And that will let you indulge, from time to time, in more expensive foods.

There is no reason to settle for second best, even if you are on a restricted budget. If you learn to spend your funds wisely, you can eat as well as anyone.

Sharpen Your Knives

One factor that can restrict a person's ability to cook at home can be the lack of proper cooking equipment. Most apartments and homes in this country come equipped with a refrigerator, stove, and cabinets–but what if yours doesn't? Or what if you are a student without access to a kitchen? Is it still possible to cook?

Of course it is. In cooking, your imagination is much more important than fancy equipment. So let's imagine that you have no cooking utensils at all, and that you will be able to spend no more than $25 a month on utensils for each of the next 6 months. How should you do it?

My first purchase would be an electric wok. With the exception of roast turkey, you can cook almost every recipe in this book in a wok. You can scramble, poach, and boil eggs. You can stir fry. You can deep fry. You can steam. And, if necessary, you can even eat with the utensils that come with the wok. Best of all, you should be able to get one for $25. If you feel it is politically incorrect to have a wok, at least get an electric skillet ($30).

My second acquisition would be a toaster-broiler oven. This gives you the ability to toast bread and bake or broil dishes. You ought to be able to get a good one for $35 to $40.

This leaves $15 for the third purchase. I would probably buy a portable Hibachi grill, allowing me to grill meats and other foods over charcoal. Of course, you cannot use one of these indoors. But a good indoor option is a bistro grill, which operates electrically–$22.

I can now cook almost every kind of food. During

the last three months, therefore, I would probably buy items like a blender ($34), dishes and utensils ($15), a crockpot ($50), or a drip coffee maker ($22). Or, it may be more feasible to save the money and buy a small, office-sized refrigerator.

Of course, if your home comes equipped with stove, oven, and refrigerator, your wish list would be quite different. You might want to save up for a microwave ($99) or perhaps even a small freezer ($180), if you plan to do a lot of bulk buying. If not–or if you do not need these items–then your $25 a month can be invested in slowly building up the tools you need to cook–and eat–well. Dishes. Pots and pans. Knives. Mixing bowls.

The approach to take in buying these items depends upon your circumstances. One person can easily get along with one plate, a bowl, a glass, a mug, and one setting of knife, fork, and spoon. Until you can afford better, you can use the same fork and spoon that you eat with to beat or stir your food as it cooks. That means you need a paring knife and a slicing knife for cooking. If you have a microwave, you may be able to use some of your eating dishes for cooking. Soup, for instance, can be fixed in the bowl you will eat it from. By washing your dishes after each use, you will find that a very few basic items can go a long way.

Of course, as your circumstances improve, you would want to expand a little, adding more dishes to eat with and more utensils to cook with. But as a general rule, do not buy any kitchen utensils until you need them. A colander may be handy if you are fixing spaghetti, but why buy it two months before you end up using it?

Some utensils can be dispensed with entirely. Many cooks cannot imagine getting by without a potato peeler, but I rarely use one. I prefer to leave the skins on the potato! Do not be intimidated into buying a lot of gadgets, especially if you cannot afford them. Buy only those that will truly help you in the actual preparation of food.

Professional chefs may find it impossible to exist without 8 high carbon steel knives and such culinary exotica as larding needles and a food mill. But I rarely use more than a paring knife and a slicing knife in preparing any meal–and I have never used larding needles or a food mill. You don't need to, either.

If you follow my advice and don't buy canned goods, you may not even need a can opener! So don't buy one until you know you are going to need it.

Warehouse clubs are good places to buy expensive items cheaply–a microwave, a freezer, or a blender. If you need to buy dishes and glassware, see if there is a glassware outlet store in your area. You can easily save 50 percent on the cost of most kitchen utensils at these outlet stores.

I adopt a similar philosophy when it comes to stockpiling staples–items such as spices, cereals, canned goods, ketchup, pickles, flour, sugar, and so on. In a good many cases, you can make your own condiments–you don't need to buy them at all. In other cases, wait until you need an item before purchasing it.

I almost never have catsup on hand, for instance–I don't care for it. If a recipe calls for it, I use a dab of tomato paste instead.

You may be able to save a lot of money if you can buy some of these staples in bulk. It doesn't make a lot of sense for one person to buy a 5-pound tub of peanut butter, but it can be very economical for a family with two kids. Instead of spending 14 or 15 cents an ounce, you can bring the cost down to 8 cents an ounce.

If you can buy in these quantities, then shopping at

a warehouse club can be a great boon to you. A three-pound can of coffee can cost as little as 1 cent a serving. A 5-pound bag of Uncle Ben's rice will cost only 4 cents a serving.

Once again, it is important to avoid succumbing to the modern American craze for convenience. It may seem practical and perhaps even economical to eat off paper plates and use plastic utensils. It certainly makes cleanup easier!   But it means you are throwing away money every time you eat.

Believe it or not, some of the costliest items in the grocery store are non-food items such as paper supplies–toilet paper, paper towels, Kleenex™, Saran Wrap™, paper napkins, and so on. You can add $20 to $30 to your shopping bill in a flash by buying these paper products. Whenever possible, it is much more cost effective to buy cloth towels, napkins, and so on that can be washed and reused.

The Japanese approach many aspects of life with the philosophy that "less is more." When I lived in Ecuador, the family I lived with did not have a single electrical kitchen appliance.   There were no paper towels or paper plates; no fancy gadgets. Just the bare minimum. But we ate well.

You can, too–no matter how tight your food budget is. Just remember that "less is more." The less you spend on gadgets, paper products, and convenience foods, the more you will have leftover to spend on food.

Get Into the Kitchen!

The big key to saving money on food is to get off the couch in the TV room and spend more time in the kitchen. We must decide that it is worthwhile to start making our own soups from scratch, instead of buying them in cans; that we can spend an extra few minutes using real rice instead of minute rice; and so on.

I grew up believing in the mighty goddess of convenience. I thought it was great to be able to pour tomato soup right out of the can into my bowl, heat it in the microwave, and then enjoy it. But then one day I made my own tomato soup. To my surprise, it wasn't hard at all. In fact, it was barely more effort than opening the can. Even more surprisingly, it tasted so much better! And I have since learned that almost all canned soups are loaded with enough salt to corrode the underside of your car. My tomato soup–in fact, all of my soups–are made with no salt at all. (Actually, with the exception of breads, where the salt acts as a leavening agent, none of my recipes call for salt. If foods are well prepared, salt should be unnecessary. If you feel any of these recipes need salt, it is probably a sign that you need to cut down on your salt consumption.)

There was one other surprise as well. Once I got hooked on making my own soups, I decided to start making my own soup stocks, whenever possible. I still keep a can or two of commercial stock on hand for emergencies, but I much prefer the chicken, beef, and vegetable stocks I make on my own. You make these stocks out of leftovers, so the cost is next to nothing. But that is not the reason I do it.

There is something magical about a pot of stock

simmering on the stove. It fills not only the kitchen but also the entire house with the most wonderful aromas. And it draws people from distant corners of the house. They have to come find out what this delightful emanation is. Soon, you have the whole family there in the kitchen with you. Talking. Interacting. Behaving like a family. In this day and age of the disintegrating nuclear family, it is wonderful to discover something that is guaranteed to bring people together. Cooking marvelous things in the kitchen will do it!

The actual amount of time you will spend preparing a basic soup stock is 10 to 15 minutes. Once it comes to a boil and you turn the heat down to simmer, your work is basically done, except for straining the soup at the end of the cooking period. But that cooking period lasts for anywhere from 30 minutes to 2 or 3 hours, depending upon your schedule. During this whole time, the house smells like a home ought to.

Almost all of the things that you can do in the kitchen to save on your food budget will also make your home a more inviting, comfortable, and livable place. Another good example of this is bread baking. You can buy a loaf of white bread for as little as 70 cents in some grocery stores, such as Cub. You can buy a loaf of oat bran or whole wheat for $1.25. These prices factor out to anywhere from 3 1/2 cents to 6 cents a slice. These figures are already so inexpensive that it may not seem worthwhile to spend time baking bread on your own, just to save a penny or two a slice. But few activities in life are more enjoyable than kneading a loaf of bread and watching it proof. And the smell of baking bread is just as powerful as the aroma of stock simmering on the stove when it comes to drawing the family into the kitchen.

This is not to imply that I would throw away my

microwave–or that I am planning to order a wood-burning stove to replace my Jenn-Aire. We just need to keep the issue of convenience in perspective. I would much rather bake potatoes for an hour in the oven than for 7 minutes in the microwave, because I get to smell them the whole time they are baking in the oven–and they taste better once they are done.

Here are some other ways you can save money on your food budget just by spending more time in the kitchen:

- Make your own salad dressings. Cut your cost from 15 cents to 3 cents a serving.
- When apples are in season and inexpensive, make your own applesauce. Either can it or freeze it for use later on.
- Make your own cranberry sauce from fresh cranberries.
- Bake your own cakes and cookies.
- Make your own pickles.
- Make your own pancake and waffle syrups.
- Make your own pasta. (You don't need expensive equipment or presses.)
- Make your own pizzas. You can do it for around $1.20 a pizza–as opposed to $3.79 or higher for a store-bought pizza. And it will taste much better.

Of course, it is not just enough to get into the kitchen more. Part of the art of stretching the food budget is knowing when to *stay* in the kitchen, once you are there. As strange as it may seem, you can often save as much money when cleaning up after a meal as you can while preparing for one. It's all a question of how you handle leftovers.

It is estimated that Americans throw away more food in the form of leftovers than many people in some other countries consume. This is a totally unnecessary

25

form of waste that needs to be eliminated, if you want to save money.

There are many things you can do with leftovers.

• Store leftover vegetables (including scraps, parings, and peelings) in a tight container in the refrigerator. Then, once a week, use these leftovers as the basis for a fresh vegetable stock. Any salad greens or other produce that are starting to wilt can be tossed into the stock, too.

• Uncooked and leftover chicken, turkey, or duck bones (and innards) can be saved for use in making chicken stock.

• Leftover beef, veal, or pork bones can be saved for use in making beef stock.

• Unused, stale bread can be used to make French toast, bread pudding, stuffing, croutons, or bread crumbs.

• If you need three egg yolks for a recipe, save the egg whites in the refrigerator until you need them–or vice-versa.

• Grind up leftover pizza in a blender or food processor, add a half pound of ground meat, and bake for an hour. Serve with tomato sauce and you have a very inexpensive but great tasting meat loaf.

• Overripe bananas can be mashed and added to muffins, quick breads, and drinks. This can be especially cost effective, if you buy ripe bananas that have been marked down for quick sale.

Breakfast

A lot of people ignore breakfast, and if your budget is tight, it may be tempting to save money by skipping this meal. In the long run, though, it is a false economy. First of all, breakfast is the most inexpensive of the three meals anyway. Second, where is the economy of saving 40 cents on breakfast and then spending 75 cents on a doughnut or muffin at work? A good breakfast will probably save you in reduced health cost bills later in life, too.

If nothing else, at least have a bowl of cold cereal and milk. Cold cereals are one category where prepared foods are still economical. A bowl of Cheerios™ and milk will cost about 30 cents. Add a glass of juice and you are still under 45 cents. There are many mornings when this is precisely the breakfast I eat. It keeps me going easily until the noon lunch break.

The ideal breakfast, though, would include fruit, eggs, meat, and bread, giving you the nutrition and energy you need for a productive morning. As you will see, there are many different ways you can eat a breakfast of this description, yet never spend more than 50 cents.

Eggs

Eggs are one of the most economical foods available, as well as a complete source of nutrition. I can buy a dozen extra large eggs in almost any local grocery store for 6 cents apiece. You can get small or medium eggs for as little as 4 cents each, if you are willing to buy 18 or two dozen at a time. Two eggs for breakfast are a time-honored custom–and only costs 12 cents!

Here are some of the ways you can fix two eggs:

Fried. Melt a tablespoon butter or margarine in a skillet. Crack each egg and drop it out of the shell into the frying pan. Cook on medium heat until the yolks are set. Serve as is for sunny-side up, or turn the eggs and then serve immediately for over easy. For firm yolks, break the yolk as soon as you put the egg in the pan.

Scrambled. Beat the eggs together in a bowl until light and frothy; add a splash or two of milk or cream. Pour mixture into pan in which you have melted a tablespoon of butter or margarine. Stir eggs with a spoon or spatula until cooked to your preference. For variety, add a strip of cooked bacon cut into little pieces (5 cents), little pieces of cooked ham (7 cents), or crumbled cooked sausage. Add a handful of grated cheese (10 cents) for cheesy eggs. Or flavor the eggs with herbs such as rosemary or tarragon.

Scrambled eggs can also be cooked in a foam cup in a microwave. Stir every 30 seconds until done. Use one cup per egg.

Shirred. Carefully crack two eggs into a small

ramekin or baking dish. Cover with two tablespoons of light or heavy cream. Top with grated cheese and some crumbled rosemary. Bake in a 400° oven 5 or 6 minutes, until set. The dish will be very hot—but oh so good!

Total cost: 20 cents.

For an extra treat, put a layer of leftover mashed potatoes or hash browns in the bottom of the baking dish before adding the eggs. Make a slight indentation in the potatoes with a spoon where you want the eggs to sit. Then proceed as before, allowing extra baking time for the potatoes. Add: 10 cents.

Soft-boiled eggs: Place eggs in a small saucepan and cover with water. Bring water to a boil over high heat. Let water boil 30 seconds, then remove the pan from the heat. Let it sit 5 minutes. Serve immediately.

Because stoves heat at different rates and people have different tastes in soft-boiled eggs, you may have to adjust the amount of time the eggs sit before serving to suit your needs.

For hard-boiled eggs, leave the eggs in the hot water for 30 to 40 minutes. Then submerge them in cold water to stop cooking.

Poached eggs: You can use an egg poacher—or just an ordinary skillet. Butter the bottom of the skillet and place on low heat. Bring a pot of water to a boil; cook eggs 10 seconds. Pour boiling water into skillet; crack eggs gently into the boiling water. Let the eggs cook in simmering water until the yolk is set but still runny. Lift eggs out of water with a slotted spoon, let drain, and then serve on a piece of toast.

It is hard to imagine anything more wonderful than poached eggs on toast. And you can fix them for only 16 cents a serving!

Generally speaking, meats are one of the most expensive of all food items. However, breakfast is a time when you can have a small portion of meat at low cost and feel as though you are eating a hearty meal.

Here are some of the more popular breakfast meats:

Bacon. Bacon can be fried over low heat, baked, or cooked in the microwave. Be sure to save the leftover bacon grease in a jar in the refrigerator; it is a flavorful substitute for oil in many dishes, and doesn't cost anything extra!

For convenience, fry up a whole pound of bacon at once, storing the unused slices in the refrigerator. They will then be ready for a quick reheating before being used in a BLT, an omelet, or even a main course.

Cost: 5 cents a slice.

Sausage. Whether links or patties, cook breakfast sausage over low heat until thoroughly cooked. Sausage can also be prepared in the microwave. Cost: 15 cents an ounce (one link or one patty).

Canadian bacon. Sauté in a tablespoon of butter until nicely browned. Cost: 20 to 40 cents, depending on how thickly it is cut.

Ham. Prepare the same as Canadian bacon.

Sausage biscuits cost 50 cents each at the store. You can make better ones for 8 cents each.

Potatoes

The average American does not usually need the starchiness of potatoes for breakfast. But if you are getting up extra early and need breakfast to last an hour or two longer than normal, adding potatoes is an inexpensive way to do it. Here are some ideas:

Hash browns. Melt two tablespoons of bacon fat in a large skillet. Grate two potatoes, skin and all; spread potatoes in an even layer over entire surface of the skillet, pressing them down with a spatula. Cook over medium heat for 6 to 7 minutes. Cut potatoes into two semicircles with edge of spatula; flip each half over. Cook until potatoes are crisp and brown. Serves two at a cost of 10 cents each.

Variations: add a half cup grated onion to potatoes before putting potatoes in the skillet. Adds 5 cents.

Add a slice of cheese or a handful of grated cheese on top of potatoes just before serving; allow it to melt. Adds: 8 cents.

Add a splash of light cream to potatoes just after turning them. Adds: 5 cents.

Appotatoes. Butter a 1 quart baking pan. Slice two potatoes and two tart apples very thin. (You can use apple sauce if you prefer.) Spread alternating layers of potatoes and apples in the dish, adding a couple of dots of butter for each layer. Beat two eggs with a half cup of milk; pour over potatoes and apples. Bake for 40 minutes in a 350° oven, until potatoes are tender. If desired, top with grated cheddar cheese and brown. Serves four. Cost: 30 cents a serving.

2 cups all-purpose flour
1/2 tsp. salt
3 tbsp. sugar
1 tbsp. baking powder
3 eggs
3 tbsp. melted butter or margarine
1 1/4 cup milk

Sift or stir together thoroughly the first four ingredients. Separate the eggs, adding the yolks to the milk and melted butter. Mix the dry and wet ingredients until a batter is formed. Whip the eggs whites until stiff, then fold into the batter. Drop the batter by spoonfuls onto a hot, greased griddle. Cook until the bubbles start to pop, then flip the cakes and brown the other sides. Serve with butter and syrup. Serves 4 at a cost of 12 cents a serving.

Variations: Substitute a half cup of rye flour, whole wheat flour, or cornmeal for a half cup of white flour.
Add a teaspoon of cinnamon to the batter.
When the pancakes are first placed on the griddle, carefully add 2 or 3 spoonfuls of blueberries, raspberries, strawberries, diced apples, sliced bananas, or chopped peaches to the top of each cake. Or, mix a few spoonfuls of applesauce or other fruit sauces to the batter before griddling. Or, try raisins or currants.

To make crepes, add an extra egg and an extra cup of milk to the pancake batter; eliminate baking powder and sugar. Refrigerate at least an hour.
Makes 32 crepes at 2 cents each.

Waffles

2 cups all-purpose flour
1/2 tsp. salt
3 tbsp. sugar
1 tbsp. baking powder
nutmeg
3 eggs
4 tbsp. melted butter or margarine
1 1/2 cup milk

Sift or stir together thoroughly the first five ingredients. Separate the eggs, adding the yolks to the milk and melted butter. Mix the dry and wet ingredients until a batter is formed. Whip the eggs whites until stiff, then fold into the batter. Drop the batter by spoonfuls onto a hot, greased waffle iron. Cook until both sides are lightly browned. Serve with butter and syrup or cinnamon sugar. Serves 4 at a cost of 12 cents a serving. The best waffles you'll ever taste!

Instead of buying syrups in the grocery store, you can make your own and save money. Try one of these:

Plain Syrup: Combine 1/4 cup each of sugar, brown sugar, and water in a saucepan. Bring to boil. Stir constantly until sugar is dissolved. If desired, add a spoonful of honey or fruit preserves to the finished syrup.
Cost: 3 cents a serving.

Fancy Syrup: Melt 5 tbsp. butter in a small pan. Stir in 1 cup heavy cream, 3 tbsp. sugar, and 1 tsp. cinnamon. Stir and heat until sugar is dissolved. Serves 10 at 9 cents a serving. Keep in refrigerator between uses.

Perfect Popovers

1 cup flour
1/4 tsp. salt
2 eggs
1 cup milk
1 tbsp. melted butter or margarine

Sift or stir together thoroughly the flour and salt. In another bowl, lightly beat the eggs. Add the milk and butter, beating until smooth. Stir liquids into the flour mixture. Stir until smooth.

Lightly butter the cups in a popover baker (or 8 glass custard cups). Fill cups to half full. Place in a cold oven. Heat oven to 425°. Bake for 35 minutes or until popovers have risen above top of the cups. Avoid opening oven door while popping! Serve with butter and syrup.

Serves four at a cost of 8 cents a serving.

You can fix the batter the night before, pour it into the cups, then refrigerate. The next morning, pop them into the cold oven and let them start popping!

Weekday Breakfast Menu

2 fried eggs
2 slices of bacon
2 slices of toast
1/2 grapefruit
coffee

Total cost per serving: 37 cents

French Toast

2 eggs
1 cup milk
1/2 tsp. vanilla extract
8 slices day-old bread

Mix first three ingredients together until well blended. Dip each side of bread slice into batter; coat but do not saturate to the point where the bread gets soggy. Brown the toast on a hot buttered griddle, turning the slices halfway through cooking. Serve with butter and syrup. Or sprinkle the buttered French toast with a combination of cinnamon and sugar.

Serves 4 at 9 cents a serving.

Santa Fe Toast

3 eggs
3/4 cup milk
1/2 tsp. nutmeg
2 cups honey nut Cheerios™
8 slices day-old bread

Blend together first three ingredients. Crush cereal slightly and spread on a piece of wax paper. Dip bread into milk and egg mixture, then into cereal. Cook toast on a medium-hot buttered griddle as above.

Serves 4 at 18 cents a serving.

Strawberry Shortcake

1 3/4 cups all purpose flour
2 1/2 tsp. double-acting baking powder
1 1/4 tsp. salt
1 tbsp. sugar
1/4 cup margarine or butter
3/4 cup milk or cream
1 qt. fresh strawberries, sliced and sugared to taste

Sift or stir together thoroughly the first four ingredients. Cut in butter with a pastry blender (or fork) until dough resembles cornmeal. Stir in milk or cream. Turn dough onto a floured board. Knead lightly. Roll out gently to a thickness of 1/4 inch. Bake at 450° for 10 or 12 minutes. Cut cake into four serving portions. Slice each portion in half horizontally. Spoon one half of strawberries on bottom biscuit layer, then cover with top biscuit layer. Add rest of strawberries and serve. Serves 6 at 33 cents each.

Variations: This shortcake recipe can also be used to make biscuits. Cut circles out of the kneaded dough using an inverted glass; bake on a cookie sheet as above. Cost per biscuit: 2 cents.

If strawberries are not in season, fresh peaches also make a delicious shortcake. Use one peach per person. Cost of peach shortcake: 20 cents a serving.

This shortcake is so hearty it can be served as a complete breakfast. Or, if served with a salad, it can make a lunch or light supper. It is guaranteed to be a hit whenever it is served.

Fried Apples & Bacon

4 winesap apples
1/4 cup water
8 slices of bacon
1/3 cup sugar

Fry the bacon over low heat until cooked but not crisp.
Remove bacon and drain off all but a couple of tablespoons of the bacon fat. Add sliced apples. Cover and
cook over low heat until apples are almost tender. Add
sugar and cook on medium heat until candied. Return
bacon to the pan and cook briefly, turning frequently.
Serves 4 at a cost of 25 cents a serving.

Weekend Breakfast Menus

#1
Fried Apples & Bacon
Popovers
Coffee

Cost per serving: 34 cents.

#2
French Toast
Homemade Sausage
Orange Juice
Coffee

Cost per serving: 31 cents.

Cereals

Oatmeal cooks up so easily it is silly to buy it in the individual serving packages so common today; all you are paying for is packaging and advertising, not food.

For four servings of oatmeal, combine 1 1/2 cups of quick oats with 3 cups of water in a glass dish. Heat on high in a microwave, stirring every minute until it reaches desired consistency. Or bring water to a boil in a pan. Stir in oats and return to a boil. Reduce heat and cook one minute, stirring occasionally. Serve with milk and brown sugar.

Cost per serving: 8 cents.

Variations: Stir a spoonful of applesauce or mashed banana into each serving of cooked oatmeal. Or add the grated peel from a lemon or an orange. Or toss in a handful of raisins. Or, sprinkle with cinnamon.

Grits

Stir 3/4 cup quick grits into 3 cups boiling water; return to a boil. Cover and reduce heat to low. Cook 5 minutes, stirring occasionally. Turn off heat; let grits stand for five minutes. Serve with butter as a side dish to make any breakfast into a hearty one.

Serves four at 4 cents each.

Variations: Add 1 cup of grated cheese, pepper to taste, a dash of nutmeg, and 2 tablespoons of butter. Or, if you need to open your eyes in a hurry, serve grits with a hot sauce on the side.

Hasty Pudding (Mush)

1 cup corn meal
1 egg yolk
2 tbsp. milk
bread crumbs or crushed Cheerios™

Boil 3 cups of water in the top of a double boiler (or in a microwave). Combine corn meal with 1 1/2 cups cold water. Stir gradually into boiling water. Cook on high heat 3 minutes, stirring constantly. Cover and steam on low heat another 15 minutes. Pour into a greased loaf pan to cool. Cut cooled mush into thick slices (3/4-inch). Beat egg yolk with milk. Dip mush slices into milk, then coat with crumbs. Fry in bacon fat or butter until crisp and golden. Serve with syrup. Serves 6 at 3 cents each.

Variations: Add Parmesan cheese and paprika and sauté it in olive oil and you can call it *polenta*.

Scrapple

Prepare mush as above. Near the end of the steaming process, add 1 1/3 pounds of cooked pork sausage, crumbled, or finely chopped pork leftovers, two chopped green onions, lightly sautéed, 1 teaspoon each of sage and marjoram, 1/4 teaspoon of thyme, and 1/2 teaspoon black pepper. Turn into greased loaf pan; let cool. Slice and fry in bacon fat. Serves 8 at 33 cents a serving.

Toad in the Hole

Prepare batter for Perfect Popovers (see page 34). Cook 8 sausage links over low heat until done. Cut each link in half. Stand half links on end in 10-ounce soufflé pots or ramekins. Add batter. Set ramekins on a baking sheet in a cold oven. Bake at 425° for 35 to 40 minutes, until the popovers have popped. Serve at once.

Serves 4 at 32 cents a serving.

Peeping Eggs

4 slices of bread
4 eggs
butter

Melt butter in a large skillet or griddle. Using a small juice glass, cut out a circle in the middle of each slice of bread. Leaving circle in the middle of the slice, toast each piece of bread in the skillet or griddle. After turning slices over, remove circles and reserve. Crack an egg into the hole in each piece of toast. Baste egg with more melted butter until it is properly cooked. Remove egg and toast to serving dishes. Return half-toasted circles to skillet or griddle; toast other side. Place circles gently on top of eggs. Serve.

Cost per serving: 8 cents.

All-Star Strata

12 slices of bread
3/4 lb. cheddar cheese, grated
2 cups cooked diced ham
6 eggs
3 cups milk
1 stick margarine

Remove crusts from bread; cut bread into cubes. Layer bread cubes, ham, and cheese in a buttered 8 x 12 baking dish. Combine eggs and milk, beating until smooth. Pour over bread, ham, and cheese. Refrigerate overnight. Remove from refrigerator at least one hour before baking. Bake one hour at 350°, uncovered.
Serves 6 at 50 cents a serving.

Homemade Sausage

1 lb. ground pork
1 tsp. sugar
1/2 tsp. red pepper
1 tsp. dried thyme
1 tsp. dried sage
1/2 tsp. pepper
Dash of allspice

Mix all ingredients together; let sit, covered, overnight in the refrigerator. Shape into patties; cook over low heat until cooked through. Cost: 8 cents a patty.

Biscuits. Use recipe for shortcake on page 36. Serve as is or top with homemade sausage for sausage biscuits (8 cents apiece) or ham and scrambled eggs for a complete meal (30 cents apiece).

Muffins. Combine 2 cups flour with 2 tablespoons sugar, 1 tablespoon baking powder, and 1 teaspoon salt. Beat 1 egg lightly and combine it with 1 cup milk and 1/4 cup vegetable oil. Add liquid to dry ingredients, stirring until just moistened. Spoon into buttered muffin pans, filling each cup two-thirds full. Bake at 400° for 20 to 25 minutes. Makes 12 muffins at 3 cents each.

Variations: Add 3/4 cup fresh blueberries to batter.

Add 3/4 cup fresh cranberries to batter.

Add 1/4 teaspoon nutmeg to batter. When done, dip each muffin top first into a small dish with 1/2 cup melted butter, then into another one with 1/2 cup sugar blended with 1 teaspoon cinnamon.

Add 1/2 cup mashed bananas or pumpkin to batter.

Add 1/2 cup chocolate chips and 1/4 cup chopped pecans to batter.

Toast. Morning toast becomes extra special when enhanced in one of the following ways:

Cinnamon Toast. Mix 1 tablespoon sugar with 1/8 teaspoon cinnamon. Sprinkle over 2 slices of buttered toast. Broil in toaster oven, until sugar melts.

Banana Toast. Peel a banana, cut in half, and cut each half into 3 slices. Sauté in 2 tablespoons butter over low heat, one minute on each side. Place banana slices on 2 pieces of buttered toast. Top with a teaspoon of sugar mixed with a pinch of nutmeg.

Mushroom Delight

1/2 lb. mushrooms
4 tbsp. margarine or butter
3/4 cup heavy cream
2 tbsp. dry sherry
4 slices buttered toast

Remove tips of mushroom stems (save for stock) and slice caps in half. Sauté mushrooms over medium heat in the butter for just a few minutes. Add cream and sherry, stirring briefly until cream is hot. Spoon over toast.

Serves 4 at 38 cents a serving.

Baked Grapefruit

2 grapefruit
2 tbsp. brown sugar
2 tbsp. dry sherry

Cut each grapefruit in half. With a grapefruit knife, loosen the flesh of the fruit from the membranes, leaving each section in its proper place. Top each half with brown sugar and broil until sugar melts. Sprinkle with sherry and serve.

Serves 4 at 13 cents a serving.

Eggs Benedict

1/2 cup Hollandaise (see page 149)
8 eggs
8 slices of Canadian bacon
4 tbsp. butter
4 homemade English muffins

Poach eggs as directed on page 29. Sauté Canadian bacon as directed on page 30. Split English muffins with a fork and toast the halves. Place two toasted halves on a plate, topping each half with one slice of Canadian bacon, one poached egg, and a dollop of Hollandaise.

Enjoy one of the pinnacles of gourmet cooking.

Serves four at 86 cents a serving.

Breakfast Burritos

8 tortillas (see page 139)
1/2 cup shredded manchego cheese (or Cheddar)
salsa
8 eggs
1/2 cup diced ham
1/4 cup chopped green onions
jalapeño pepper slices

Scramble eggs, ham, green onions, and salsa to taste. Cook over low heat. When cooked to desired consistency, spoon on to tortillas. Roll up, place in baking dish, and cover with cheese and jalapeño pepper slices. Broil until cheese is melted.

Serves 4 at 27 cents each.

Lunches & Light Suppers

Lunch is usually a very informal meal. It may be eaten out of a paper bag or a lunch box. It may be hot or cold. Often, it is an opportunity to use up leftovers. It deserves, however, to be something more than a peanut butter sandwich—and still be inexpensive.

Actually, lunch provides us with lots of examples of how we are apt to waste money in our quest for convenience. Several food companies have come out with a highly packaged "lunch kit" that includes lunch meat, cheeses, crackers, a dessert, and a beverage—all for $2.29. But $2.29 is a far cry from the 80 cents that the average lunch costs when prepared with the recipes in this book.

Keep in mind that lunch is not necessarily the midday meal. Many of the recipes that follow are quite suitable served as the core of a light supper, or even more. Snert, for example—a Dutch version of what we call split pea soup—is served in Holland as an evening meal after the family has been out ice skating on the canals all afternoon. It is perhaps the original crock pot meal!

Making soup begins with making your own stocks.

Vegetable stock. Sauté two or three chopped green onions in a large pot. Add 1/2 cup each of diced carrots and celery; any leftover salad greens; and your collection of leftover vegetables from the week. Toss in a few pinches of salad or soup herbs, a dash of cayenne pepper, and a strong shaking of black pepper. Cover with cold water and bring to a boil. Reduce heat, cover, and simmer for 30 minutes to 2 hours. Pour stock through a sieve. Cost: 3 cents per cup of stock.

An alternative is simply to save the broth left over from cooking vegetables in a refrigerator container. Cost: 0 cents. Or, for the best possible broth, use this saved liquid as part of the water in the recipe above.

Chicken stock: Follow the same procedure as above, but substitute uncooked chicken scraps for the leftover vegetables and greens. Use tarragon, thyme, and dill-weed in lieu of salad herbs. Simmer at least one hour. After stock has been sieved, refrigerate it. The fat will rise to the top and harden, making it easy to remove.

If you do not have chicken scraps, buy two pounds of chicken breasts and wings. When the stock is done, remove the meat from the bones and skin, dice it, and save it for use in chicken salad and other recipes. Or use turkey instead of chicken. Cost of stock: 2 cents a cup.

Beef stock. Save the broth created by cooking a pot roast, or rouladen. Or buy beef scraps at your grocery and boil them down in the same fashion as for chicken. Use parsley and a bay leaf instead of tarragon and dill.

Curried Lima Bean Soup

10 oz. package frozen baby lima beans
3 green onions
2 cups of half and half
2 tbsp. butter
1 tsp. curry powder
1/4 tsp. marjoram
1 cup vegetable or chicken broth
pepper

Sauté chopped green onions in butter in pot. Add lima beans, curry powder, marjoram, pepper, and broth. Bring to a boil, cover, reduce heat, and simmer for 15 minutes. Purée for 5 or 6 seconds in a blender. Return vegetables to pot, add half and half. Serve hot or cold.
Serves 4 at 27 cents a serving.

Brown Chow Stew

6 cups beef or turkey broth
4 carrots, sliced
3 potatoes, diced
1 head of shredded cabbage
1/2 lb. cooked beef or turkey, sliced thinly

Simmer all ingredients together for at least one hour. Top each serving with toasted croutons. Serves 6 at 35 cents (turkey) or 40 cents (beef) a serving.

Tomato Soup

2 cups vegetable or chicken broth
1 can plum tomatoes (15 ounces)
1 tsp. basil
1 tsp. garlic flakes
2 tbsp. margarine or butter
pepper

Chop tomatoes. Combine with broth, the liquid from the can, basil, and garlic and bring to a boil. Reduce heat. Simmer for 20 to 30 minutes on the stove, or cook for 7 minutes in a microwave. Stir in butter; add pepper. Serves 4 at 13 cents a serving.

Variation: Swirl in 1/2 cup heavy cream instead of the butter for cream of tomato soup. Adds 7 cents.

Snert (Dutch Pea Soup)

1 lb. split peas
one bunch of leeks, cleaned and chopped
1 stalk of celery, chopped
2 medium onions, peeled and chopped
1 cup light cream
1 cup diced ham
5 cups vegetable or chicken broth
3 tbsp. margarine or butter

Bring split peas and broth to boil; simmer 30 minutes. Add vegetables and ham; simmer 30 minutes more. Swirl in cream and butter. Serve.

Serves 6 at 34 cents per serving

Cream of Carrot Soup

2 cups chicken or vegetable broth
1 cup finely chopped carrots
1 bunch chopped green onions
1/4 cup chopped fresh parsley
1 cup cream

Simmer first four ingredients for 30 minutes. Purée cooked broth and vegetables in a blender for 5 to 6 seconds. Return to pot. Add cream and bring to serving temperature.

Serves 4 at 20 cents a serving.

Variations: Substitute cauliflower, celery, broccoli, onion, peas, or spinach for the carrots.

Corn Chowder

3 slices cooked bacon
2 medium potatoes
1 1/2 cups creamed corn
1 chopped onion
2 cups light cream
A pinch of thyme
paprika

Boil potatoes about 15 minutes, or until cooked but still firm. Sauté the onion until limp; add bacon, potatoes, and potato broth. Bring to boil, then simmer for 10 minutes. Stir in corn and cream. Heat to serving temperature. Stir in thyme. When serving, sprinkle each bowl with paprika. Serves 4 at 46 cents each.

Vichyssoise

3 medium leeks
1 onion
2 tbsp. butter
4 medium potatoes
4 cups chicken or vegetable stock
2 cups cream
1/4 tsp. mace

Sauté minced leeks and onions briefly in the butter. Add sliced potatoes and stock. Bring to a boil, reduce heat, and simmer for 15 to 30 minutes. Purée in a blender for 5 to 6 seconds. Stir in cream and mace. Chill to serve cold, or reheat to serve warm.
Serves 6 at 45 cents a serving.

Shrimp Bisque

2/3 lb. green shrimp
6 tbsp. margarine
2 tbsp. grated onion
4 cups half and half
nutmeg and chives
3 tbsp. sherry

Peel and clean shrimp. Cook in microwave until almost done, checking every 20 seconds. Mince. Melt butter in microwave; cook onion for two minutes. Add shrimp and half and half; cook slowly until thoroughly heated. Do not boil. Add nutmeg and chives. Swirl in sherry.
Serves 4 at $1.10 a serving.

Salads

A salad can be as simple as a wedge of iceberg lettuce smothered with mayonnaise (cost: 10 cents), or as complicated as human imagination–and the budget–will allow. The important thing is that salads can provide a lot of eating enjoyment and food value very inexpensively. The best place to buy salad fixings is usually at a farmers market. If you have a refrigerator, buy enough to last a week. At the end of the week, toss anything left over into your vegetable stock pot.

You can also save a lot of money by making your own salad dressings.

Banana Nut Salad

4 bananas
4 leaves of leaf lettuce
mayonnaise
chopped walnuts or pecans

Peel bananas and slice in half lengthwise. Lay two halves on each leaf of lettuce. Smother flat side of each banana slice with mayonnaise. Sprinkle top with nuts.

Serves 4 at 15 cents a serving.

Mayonnaise: Mix two egg yolks with 1 teaspoon dry mustard and a dash of cayenne. Stir in 3 tablespoons of lemon juice. Beat in 1/2 cup of salad oil a few drops at a time, then beat in another 1 1/2 cups of oil a bit more rapidly (use a hand mixer or blender if you have one). Cost: 4 cents an ounce.

3 C Salad

2 small canteloupes
2 cups cold cooked chicken, cubed
1/4 cup celery, thinly sliced
1/4 cup green onions, chopped
1/4 cup red or green pepper
1/4 cup chopped peanuts

Cut canteloupes in half, scoop out seeds, and remove the fruit of the melon with a melon ball cutter or knife. Mix the chicken, celery, onions, and pepper. Stir in curry dressing and melon balls. Refrigerate. To serve, spoon melon-chicken mixture into empty canteloupe shells and sprinkle with nuts. Serves 4 at 65 cents each.

Curry dressing: In a blender, mix until smooth: 1/3 cup peanut butter, 1/3 cup mayonnaise, and 1/3 cup sour cream; 2 tablespoons lime juice; 1 teaspoon garlic flakes; 1 teaspoon curry powder; 1/4 teaspoon ginger; and 1/4 teaspoon soy sauce.

Egg and Avocado Salad

2 avocados
4 hard-boiled eggs
curry powder
mayonnaise (see page 51)

Peel eggs and chop finely. Mix with mayonnaise and curry powder to taste. Slice avocados in half lengthwise; remove pit. Spoon egg salad into avocados and serve. Makes 4 servings at 32 cents apiece.

Taco Salad

1 lb. ground beef or strips of flank steak
1 onion, chopped
1 can kidney beans (15 oz.)
1 1/2 tsp. chili powder
1/2 tsp. cumin
1/2 cup catsup
1 cup shredded Cheddar or Asadero cheese
2 avocados, peeled, pitted, and sliced
1 head iceberg lettuce, shredded
2 ripe tomatoes, cut in wedges
4 hard boiled eggs, cut in wedges
chopped green onion

Sauté meat and onion over medium high heat until browned; drain off drippings. Stir in beans, chili powder, cumin, and catsup. Simmer on low heat 5 minutes.

Arrange lettuce on 4 large plates. Top with beef, cheese, tomato and egg wedges, and chopped green onion. Finish with a dollop of sour cream in the middle, surrounded by tortilla chips. Makes a complete meal at 90 cents a serving (ground beef) or $1.40 (flank steak).

Cole Slaw

1/4 head green cabbage, shredded in long strips
1/8 head red cabbage, shredded in long strips
1/2 cup shredded carrot

Toss shredded ingredients; dish onto serving plates. Top with slaw dressing (see page 149) and serve.

Serves 4 for 8 cents each.

Crab Louis

1 cup mayonnaise (see page 51)
1/4 cup catsup
1/2 tsp. chili powder
1/4 cup each chopped green pepper & green onion
1/4 cup heavy cream, whipped
2 lemons
1 head iceberg lettuce
1 lb. imitation or real crab meat
4 ripe tomatoes, cut in wedges
4 hard-cooked eggs, cut in wedges

Make Louis dressing by mixing mayonnaise, catsup, chili powder, green pepper and onion; fold into whipped cream. Add juice of one lemon to taste.

Shred lettuce and arrange on four plates. Mound crabmeat in center of lettuce. Surround crabmeat with tomato and egg wedges. Top with dressing and garnish with a lemon wedge. Cost per serving: $1.10.

Waldorf Salad

1 large apple
1 cup seedless red grapes
1 cup diced celery
1/2 cup chopped walnuts
1/2 cup mayonnaise

Mix all ingredients. Chill at least one hour. Serves 4 at 25 cents each.

Plum Good Salad

4 plums
one head bibb lettuce
1/3 cup mayonnaise
3 tsp. tarragon white wine vinegar
3/4 tsp. sugar
1/3 cup heavy cream

Blend together mayonnaise, vinegar, and sugar; fold into whipped cream. Arrange sliced plums on a layer of lettuce on each plate; top with dressing. Sprinkle with crushed tarragon. Serves 4 at 60 cents each.

Potato Salad

5 large redskin potatoes
5 tsp. parsley flakes or 1/3 cup fresh parsley
1 small onion, minced
1 tbsp. Dijon mustard
3/4 tsp. tarragon
1/2 tsp. minced garlic
1/2 cup tarragon white wine vinegar
2/3 cup salad oil

Simmer potatoes in one inch boiling water for 30 minutes. Drain and cool, then slice. Place potatoes, parsley, and onion in a large bowl. Blend mustard, tarragon, garlic, vinegar, and oil. Coat potatoes with oil, tossing gently. Let stand at room temperature for 3 hours. Chill. Serves 8 at 15 cents each.

Omelets

There is no greater triumph of gourmet cooking than a perfect omelet. And a perfect omelet costs just 20 cents a serving if made with three eggs, 14 cents if made with two eggs.

Crack the eggs into a bowl and beat them with a fork, a spoon, a wire whisk, or a beater. Add a splash of milk or cream and continue beating until smooth and creamy. Heat a small skillet over high heat. As soon as it is hot, swirl one pat of butter or margarine to cover the entire bottom. Immediately add the beaten eggs. Cook over high heat, shoving the cooked part of the egg into the center and tilting the pan so that the uncooked egg runs into the bare spots, thereby cooking faster. The entire omelet should cook in just one minute. Tilt the pan so that the omelet slides about an inch up the side; add any filling at this point. *Do not brown or overcook the omelet.* Fold omelet over itself to make a half moon; then drop on the serving plate.

Fillings: A handful of grated cheese. The cheese will melt as it contacts the hot egg. Add 10 cents.

A quarter cup of any chopped cooked meat, slightly rewarmed–ham, chicken, pork, turkey, or beef.

Two or three sliced mushrooms that have been lightly sautéed in butter.

Three tablespoonsful of chili.

Two diced cooked shrimp. Add 12 cents.

Two slices of cooked bacon. Add 12 cents.

Leftover hash browns, rewarmed. Add 4 cents.

Sautéed bits of peppers, green onions, or zucchini.

Herbs, salsa, sauces, or spices to please your taste.

Any combination of the above.

Hamburger Crunch

1 loaf homemade French bread
1 lb. ground beef
2 tbsp. Worcestershire sauce
1 small onion, chopped

Mix ground beef, Worcestershire, and chopped onion lightly together. Split bread in half lengthwise. Toast bread briefly under broiler. Remove from oven; spread bread with a thin coating of the beef mixture. Flatten beef into bread. Return bread to oven; broil until meat is cooked. Cut into serving pieces. This will be the best hamburger you've ever had. Serves 4 at 30 cents each.

Variation: Add slices of your favorite cheese after beef is cooked. Melt and serve. Add 10 cents.

Lunch Menus

#1
Hamburger Crunch
Potato Salad
Iced Tea
Cost: 57 cents

#2
Cream of Carrot Soup
3 C Salad
Iced Tea
Cost: 97 cents

3/4 lb. ground beef
1/3 cup chopped green onions
1/3 cup chopped green pepper
2 tbsp. butter
1/3 cup chopped mushrooms
3 tbsp. chili sauce or salsa
4 hamburger buns

Sauté onions and pepper in butter. Add beef, cooking until lightly browned. Add mushrooms and chili sauce. Cover and simmer until mushrooms are cooked. Serve on toasted buns. Serves 4 at 43 cents each.

Variation: Serve in taco shells or burritos with salsa, cheese, and guacamole–"Sloppy Josés."
Cost: 50 cents each.

Add a can of kidney beans and a couple of chopped tomatoes to the first 6 ingredients and you have the makings of a good bowl of chili. Top with some grated manchego cheese, chopped green onions, a dollop of sour cream, and taco chips.
Cost: 69 cents a serving.

Chili Sauce: Add 1 teaspoon or more chili powder to 1 cup of catsup. Blend well. Cost: 2 cents an ounce.

Salsa: Add 1 minced jalapeño pepper, 1 chopped green onion, 1 tsp. minced garlic, 1/2 cup chopped tomato, and 1/8 cup minced green pepper to 1 cup catsup. Blend well. To increase heat, add more jalapeño peppers to taste. Cost: 5 cents an ounce.

Fillups

Fillups are any kind of wrapping that let you insert fillings. Pita bread, tacos, and tortillas are great fillups. You can also take dough for crescent rolls, roll it flat, cut it into rectangles, spoon on a filling, roll them up, and bake them. Or do the same thing with filo dough. Or crepes. Just make sure the fillings are fully cooked.

Steak Fillups. Sauté or grill 1/2 pound of flank steak over high heat. Slice thinly. Continue cooking to desired level. Chop into bite sized pieces. Add equal amounts of meat to four pitas or tacos. If using pitas, add shredded lettuce, feta cheese, chopped tomatoes, and ranch dressing. If using taco shells, add shredded lettuce, shredded cheese, chopped tomatoes, and salsa. Cost: 75 cents each.

Veal Oscar Fillups. Sauté 1/3 pound of veal cube steak, cut in thin strips, with 1 chopped green onion and 1/2 cup sliced mushrooms. Break in half stalks from 1/4 pound fresh asparagus; save woody ends for soup. Slice tip ends in thin diagonal slices; sauté quickly with veal. Add 3 ounces crab meat. Spoon mixture onto crepes, filo dough, or roll ups. In case of crepes, roll up, top with bearnaise sauce and serve. In case of filo or roll ups, bake 12 to 15 minutes in a 350° oven. Top with bearnaise and serve. Cost: 90 cents each.

Filo Fillups. Dampen one flat sheet of filo dough lightly with butter. Add another sheet and butter; then two more. Add 1/2 cup cooked diced ham and 1/4 cup cooked chopped asparagus; spoon on bearnaise. Roll up and bake at 400° for 5 minutes. Serves 2 for 24 cents.

Hash

1/2 lb. leftover beef stew or pot roast, with gravy
1/2 lb. leftover ham
4 uncooked cubed creamer potatoes
1/4 lb. sliced mushrooms
Splash of dry sherry

Chop meats and potatoes into small cubes and combine in a skillet. Simmer for 15 minutes in the beef gravy. Add mushrooms and sherry, simmer for 15 minutes more. Serve over toast or use as filling for fillups (see page 59). Serves 4 at 90 cents each.

Chicken Hash. Substitute chicken for the meats in the recipe above. Add 1/2 cup light cream and a pat of butter along with the mushrooms and sherry. Sprinkle with grated Parmesan cheese before serving.
Cost: 66 cents a serving.

Red Flannel Hash. Use 1 pound ground chuck instead of the meat or chicken, and replace 2 of the 4 potatoes with 2 beets. Sauté 1 chopped onion in 4 tablespoons of butter; add hash and cook for 10 minutes over medium-low heat. Transfer to a baking dish. Combine 1 tablespoon cream with 4 tablespoons butter, drizzle over top of hash. Broil for 5 minutes until top forms rich crust.
If you like, serve with a poached egg on top of each portion.
Cost: 55 cents a serving.

Variation: Use turkey in any of the recipes above.

Pizza

I may never find a better pizza than that made by Donatos, a chain based in Columbus, Ohio, that has spent 30 years perfecting their pizza. But since I can no longer order a Donatos, I comfort myself with the following:

1 teaspoon yeast
3 cups all purpose flour
1/4 tsp. sugar
3 tbsp. melted butter
3/4 cup half and half
2 eggs

Dissolve yeast and sugar in 1/4 cup warm water. Let sit until frothy. Add beaten egg, melted butter, and half and half. Stir in flour, forming a ball of dough. Place dough on a floured surface and knead for 5 minutes. Place ball in an oiled bowl, cover with a towel, and let rise until dough has doubled in bulk (45 minutes). Punch down dough, split in half. Roll out each half to 13-inch circle. Transfer dough to two 12-inch pans, doubling back edges to form thick rim. Cover with towel; let rise for 15 minutes. Bake 10 minutes in 450° oven, then add desired toppings:

3 cups tomato cream sauce (see page 149).
Grated mozzarella, romano, and Parmesan cheeses
Sliced pepperoni
Sautéed sliced mushrooms, onions, green peppers
Crumbled cooked Italian sausage

Bake another 15 minutes. Serves 8 at 30 cents each.

Homemade Beans & Franks

Why go to all this trouble for something you can buy in a can? Because canned beans are dull and over-processed. And if you cook beans from scratch you get to smell the wonderful aroma for half a day.

1 1/2 cups dried beans
1/4 cup chopped onion
2 tbsp. dark molasses
2 tbsp. catsup
1 tbsp. dry mustard
1/2 cup beer
1/4 lb. sliced salt pork
3/4 lb. franks

Cover beans with water. Bring to boil, simmer for one hour. Drain beans, saving water for vegetable broth. Add next five ingredients. Place in greased casserole, dot with salt pork. Bake in 250° oven for 6 to 8 hours. Add franks. Bake another 30 minutes. Uncover and bake another 30 minutes. Serves 4 at 30 cents each.

Light Supper Menu

Curried Lima Bean Soup
Bacon, shrimp, and cheese omelet
Appotatoes
Hot Cocoa
Supreme Shortcake
Cost: $1.50 a person

MacCrab

8 oz. macaroni
2 cups grated cheese
2 tbsp. butter
2 tbsp. flour
1 cup milk
12 oz. imitation or real crabmeat
1 minced green onion
3 tbsp. buttered bread crumbs

Boil macaroni in water as directed on package. Make cream sauce by heating together butter, flour, and milk, stirring until thickened. Place drained macaroni in a buttered baking dish in alternate layers with cheese, cream sauce, and the crabmeat mixed with the onion. Top with remaining sauce and crumbs. Bake at 350° for 20 minutes. Serves 4 at 65 cents each.

Variations: Substitute shrimp for crab, or use half of each.
Use lasagna noodles instead of macaroni, and Italian cheeses, to make seafood lasagna. You can even add a hint of tomato sauce, if desired.

Serve with a banana nut salad for an 80-cent lunch or supper.

Sandwiches

The key to a great sandwich is the right kind of bread. By making bread yourself (see pages 137 to 146), you can not only save a lot of money but also make every sandwich you serve tastier, healthier, and more exciting. The possibilities for sandwiches are, of course, virtually endless, limited only by your imagination. Here are some standard–and not so standard–suggestions:

Peanut Butter. Spread fresh-ground peanut butter on buttered or plain slices of oatmeal bread. 10 cents.
Add a leaf of lettuce between the slices. 12 cents.
Add any kind of jelly or jam. 12 cents.
ESP B&J (extra special peanut butter and jelly). Spread peanut butter on one slice, jam on the other. Top peanut butter with crushed peanuts, jam with freshly sliced strawberries or kiwi. Cost: 20 cents each.

CC & J. Thickly spread cottage cheese on a piece of bread. In the center, spoon a dollop of apricot preserves or your favorite jam. Toast under broiler until hot.
Or sprinkle the cottage cheese with cinnamon. Cost: 22 cents each.

BLT. On one piece of buttered toast, place a leaf of lettuce, two half-strips of bacon, and a slice of a large ripe tomato. Top with second piece of buttered toast. Cost: 20 cents.

BELT. Same as a BLT, but add a sliced hard-boiled egg on top of tomato. Cost: 26 cents.

Melted cheese. Lay one slice of cheddar cheese on one slice of bread, a slice of Monterey jack on the second. Toast in a toaster oven until toast is crispy, cheeses are melted. Cost: 28 cents.

Variations: add a third or fourth type of sliced cheese.

Add finely chopped olives or jalapeño peppers.

Add 2 slices of crisp, cooked bacon.

Egg sandwich: Place slices of 1 hard-boiled egg on a buttered piece of banana or cranberry bread. Eat open face. 10 cents each.

Egg salad sandwich. Spread egg salad mixture (see page 52) over one piece of bread or toast; top with another. Cost 20 cents.

Club sandwich: Toast three slices of bread. Spread each with mayonnaise. On the first slice, stack a leaf of lettuce, 3 crisp slices of bacon, a tomato slice, and toast slice #2. On toast slice #2, stack a slice of ham, a slice of turkey breast, and the last slice of toast. Cut the sandwich into quarters along the bias; secure each section with toothpicks. Cost: 85 cents.

Variation: use chicken salad instead of ham and turkey.

Shrimp and avocado sandwich. Mince 12 medium cooked shrimp. Mash one avocado. Blend with one chopped hard-boiled egg and shrimp. Spread paste onto four slices of toast. Top sandwiches with four other slices of toast.

Serves 4 at 45 cents each.

Quesadillas

If you live in a region of the U.S. where you can buy authentic Mexican cheeses–asadero, enchilada, and manchego cheeses–then use these. If not, then substitute cheddar and Monterey jack.

4 flour tortillas (see page 139)
3/4 cup grated asadero cheese
3/4 cup grated manchego cheese
4 tbsp. sliced black olives
4 tbsp. sliced jalapeño peppers
4 tbsp. salsa (see page 58)
shredded lettuce
guacamole

Cover one half of each tortilla with asadero cheese, the other half with manchego cheese. Add olives, jalapeños, and salsa. Fold tortilla to close; press down to seal. Bake at 450° for 5 minutes until cheese is melted and tortillas golden. To serve, top with shredded lettuce and guacamole, with more salsa on the side. Serves 4 at 35 cents each.

Variations: Reduce each cheese to 1/2 cup, then also add 1/2 cup of diced cooked bacon, chicken, ham, or turkey. But keep in mind that a quesadilla is, by definition, a "little cheese meal."

Fried Rice

2 cups cooked rice (see page 111)
1 tbsp. oil
1 tbsp. bacon fat
3 green onions, sliced
4 tsp. soy sauce
2 eggs
1/2 cup diced cooked meat–shrimp, chicken, ham, pork, or bacon

Heat oil and bacon fat in hot wok or skillet. Add rice. Stir rice to mix well with oil and fat. Add soy sauce; stir well. Stir in green onion. Make cavity in center of wok or pan by shoving rice to the sides. Break eggs into center cavity; scramble quickly. Do not let egg mix with rice until nearly set. Then stir the cooked pieces of egg throughout the rice mixture. Add cooked meats (or combination); heat and serve.

Makes 4 servings at 30 cents each.

If the fried rice is to be your main dish, increase the amount of cooked rice to 3 cups, use a total of 3 tablespoons oil and fat, 6 tsp. soy sauce, 4 green onions, and 1 cup of cooked meat. Add 1/4 cup cooked peas and 1/4 cup cooked diced carrots.

Makes 4 servings at 45 cents each.

Jambalaya

2 slices diced bacon
1/4 cup chopped onion
1/2 green pepper, cut in julienned strips
1 cup canned tomatoes
3 cups cooked rice
1 cup cooked cubed ham, chicken, and sausage
4 large green shrimp, still in shell
1/8 tsp. Tabasco
1 tsp. thyme or oregano

Sauté onion and green pepper with bacon. Add rice, tomatoes (and their juice), 1 cup water, Tabasco, cooked meats, and seasonings. Boil, then reduce heat and simmer for 15 minutes. Add shrimp and cook until shrimp turns pink–no longer. Serve immediately, making sure each diner gets one shrimp.

Serves 4 at 55 cents each. A meal in itself.

Deviled Eggs

12 hard-boiled eggs
mayonnaise (see page 51)
curry powder

Peel eggs and split them lengthwise. Scoop out yolks. Mix yolks with mayonnaise until you achieve desired consistency. Add curry powder to taste.

Makes 8 servings (3 halves each) at 12 cents each.
Variations: Substitute tarragon or salsa for curry.

Ravioli

Once you taste homemade ravioli, you will never go back to the can.

    2 sheets of ravioli dough (see page 146)
    1 slice leftover pizza, cut up and puréed
    1/4 cup ground beef or veal, cooked
    1 egg
    Parmesan cheese
    tomato cream sauce (see page 149)

Combine pizza, meat, and egg to form a paste. If it does not adhere completely, add cream until it does. On one sheet of dough, place a mound of filling every three inches, leaving 2-inch gaps. Lay other sheet on top, pressing down gently. Cut dough into 3-inch squares; press edges to seal. Let ravioli dry at room temperature for 2 hours. Freeze or refrigerate. When ready to serve, boil for about 10 minutes. Drain and sprinkle with Parmesan cheese. Serve with tomato cream sauce. Serves 4 for 15 cents each.

Variations: Instead of the pizza and meat, use the following fillings:

1. 2/3 cup ricotta cheese blended with a tablespoon of grated Parmesan and a tablespoon of grated mozzarella. Add a sprinkling of nutmeg to the egg. Serve with a tomato cream sauce.

2. Cook leftover asparagus stalks for 5 minutes in boiling water; purée enough to make 1/4 cup. Blend it with 1/4 cup cooked veal. Blend with egg. Serve cooked ravioli with a garnish of imitation crab and hollandaise sauce for Veal Oscar Ravioli.

4 winesap apples
4 slices bacon
1 16-oz. can creamed corn
1/2 cup sugar

Fry bacon in skillet until crisp. Remove bacon and most of drippings. Add apples, cored and sliced, and water. Cook until apples are almost tender. Add sugar and drippings, cooking until apples are brown and candied. Add corn; heat through. Serve with a slice of bacon on top of each serving. Makes 4 servings at 35 cents each.

Variation: for a heartier meal, add 4 medallions of pork to the above recipe. Sauté pork while the bacon is cooking.

ABC shortcut shortcake. Serve either version over warm split biscuits.

ABC pot pie. Cut cooked pork into thin strips. Place entire mixture in a baked pie shell; sprinkle with thyme and dot with butter. Cover with a second pie crust; slash pastry in several places, then brush with 1 beaten egg. Bake in a 350° oven for 25 to 30 minutes.

Ham Croquettes

1 cup white sauce (see page 149)
2 egg yolks
2 cups cooked ham, minced
1/4 tsp. grated onion
1/2 tsp. nutmeg
2 tbsp. chopped parsley
1 tsp. Worcestershire sauce

Stir warmed cream sauce into the egg yolks, a little at a time, stirring until blended. Add rest of ingredients and blend. Chill in a shallow baking dish. Cut chilled mixture into 12 sections and shape into balls or cones. Dip in flour, next into 1 beaten egg, and then into bread crumbs. Deep fry in 385° oil in a wok for 2 to 3 minutes, until golden. Drain on paper towels.

Makes 4 servings at 40 cents each.

Variations: Add 10 ounces of creamed corn in lieu of one cup of the ham, plus 2 tablespoons of grated green pepper.

Add grated parmesan cheese to the bread crumbs.

Substitute 2 cups of cooked chicken or turkey for the ham.

Or use 2 cups of minced shrimp and imitation crabmeat in place of the ham. Add a dash of sherry.

For a change of pace, try these croquettes as a breakfast meat dish.

Chicken Kiev Popups

1 cup minced chicken
1/2 stick butter
1 tbsp. chopped chives
1 tbsp. chopped parsley
popover batter (see page 34)

Let butter soften, then blend with chives and parsley. Form into 8 small balls. Chill. Pack chicken around each butter ball, forming 8 balls. Pour popover batter 1/4 full into each of 8 popover cups. Gently add chicken ball. Pour remaining batter into cups, but no more than half-full. Place in cold oven. Immediately heat to 425°. Cook for 35 minutes. Serves 4 at 29 cents each.

Light Supper Menus

#1
ABC Pot Pie
Plum Good Salad
Hot Tea
Icebox Pudding
Cost: $1.50

#2
Chicken Kiev Popups
Peas Majorca Style
Mashed Potatoes
Hot Tea
Pumpkin Pie
Cost: 72 cents

Entrées

Some of the most glorious entrées yet devised by the imagination of mankind are also quite inexpensive to fix. It's usually just a question of how you prepare them. Take meat loaf, as an example. The meat loaf that is served on most blue plate specials in diners throughout the country is a disgrace. But few meals are more satisfying than a good meat loaf. It is a much more creative cooking statement than a steak.

My approach to the entrées that follow is to focus primarily on inexpensive meats–a turkey or pot roast, for example–and to make more expensive meats share the spotlight with interesting and even exotic accompaniments. A great way to serve Beef Stroganoff or Veal Francaise, for example, is as the topping for a baked potato. Instead of having to serve 1/4 or 1/2 pound of meat, you can get by with just 2 ounces. And even two ounces of filet or veal can be afforded on a $1.98 budget!

All-American Turkey

1 16-lb. turkey
3/4 cup margarine or butter
3/4 cup each chopped onion and chopped celery
24 ounces creamed corn
12 ounces prepared stuffing mix (*not* cornbread)

Sauté onion and celery in butter. Add corn. Mix stuffing with water as directed on the package (1 1/2 cups). Toss stuffing with corn mixture. Let cool. Remove packet of innards from a fresh or defrosted turkey. Stuff inner cavity with stuffing mix; close skin flaps to keep stuffing inside the turkey (use short skewers or string–or large safety pins). Rub outside with butter. Cover breast with cheesecloth soaked in butter or aluminum foil. Place turkey breast-side up on a rack in a roasting pan. Bake 5 1/2 hours in a 325° oven, basting every 30 minutes with the drippings (add or subtract 20 minutes for each pound of difference). Remove cheesecloth or foil 30 minutes before done. To test for doneness, pierce a drumstick. If the juices run clear, it is done. Let sit 10 minutes while you make a gravy.

Pour drippings into a large glass measuring cup and set in freezer for 5 minutes. Remove fat that has risen to the top; return rest of liquid to saucepan. Add enough turkey broth (see page 46) made with the innards while the turkey was cooking (save cooked innards for other uses) to bring liquid to 3 cups. Bring to a boil. Strain, then add to 3 tablespoons melted butter and 3 tablespoons flour. Stir vigorously. If desired, add minced pieces of the cooked giblets. Slice turkey and serve with stuffing and fresh cranberry sauce.

Makes 24 servings at 45 cents each.

Pot Roast

3 lb. chuck roast
1 chopped carrot & 1 stalk sliced celery
1 cup dry red wine

Dredge roast in flour, then brown in 2 tablespoons butter. After 2 minutes or so, turn roast over, and add chopped vegtables. When meat is browned, remove to a roasting pan. Add two onions peeled and cut in half and 1 cup of either beef or vegetable stock and one part dry red wine. Cover and bake at 300° for 3 hours. After 90 minutes, add 4 potatoes, scrubbed and quartered. After two hours, add 4 to 6 carrots, scrubbed and quartered. Add more stock or wine if needed while baking. When done, let roast sit 10 minutes while you make a pan gravy. (Same method as for turkey.)

Makes two meals for 4 people at 80 cents (with potatoes and carrots); 65 cents for just the meat.

Beef Brisket

Trim fat from a 5 to 6-lb. fresh brisket (not corned beef). Place in a pan the size of the brisket. Sprinkle generously with paprika. Add one half a chopped onion. Cover with aluminum foil and bake at 325° for 3 hours. Leave meat in juices; refrigerate. To serve, slice very thinly across the grain with a sharp knife. Keep slices together so that brisket retains original shape. Heat meat in its juices at 325 for 30 minutes.

If you freeze what you do not eat, you should get four meals for 4 people, at $1.05 a serving.

Swiss Steak

1 1/2 lbs. round steak (4 steaks)
1/2 cup finely chopped onions
1 cup mixed chopped carrots, peppers, and celery
small can stewing tomatoes (8 ounces)
1 cup stock

With a mallet or side of a plate, pound as much flour as possible into each steak, top and bottom. Sauté quickly in bacon fat. After turning steaks over, add onions and mixed vegetables. Transfer to an oven pan, add stock and tomatoes, and bake at 300° for 2 hours. Remove steak to a hot platter; keep warm. Strain and degrease drippings, then make pan gravy (as described on page 74). Serves 4 for $1.35 each.

Creamed Chipped Beef

8 oz. chipped beef
3 tbsp. butter
3 tbsp. each minced onions & green pepper
3 tbsp. flour
2 cups milk
1 tbsp. chives and 1/4 tsp. paprika
2 tbsp. dry sherry
4 boiled white or sweet potatoes, cut in cubes

Sauté onions and peppers in butter. Sprinkle with flour. Add milk slowly, stirring constantly. Pull apart beef and add. Simmer until thicken. Remove from heat and season with chives, paprika, and sherry. Serve on potatoes. Serves 4 at 80 cents each.

Meat Loaf of the Gods

1 pound ground beef (or mixture of ground meats)
3/4 cup fresh bread crumbs
1/2 tsp. thyme
1/2 cup chopped parsley
1 egg, lightly beaten
2 tbsp. butter
3/4 cup chopped onion
1/2 cup chopped celery
4 slices bacon

Mix meat with bread crumbs, thyme, parsley, and egg in a large bowl. Sauté onion and celery in the butter in a small saucepan. Let cool, then add to the meat. Mix together by hand, then shape into an oval loaf. Place in an oval buttered pan and cover with bacon slices. Bake at 350° for an hour and a quarter. Let it sit a few minutes before slicing, or else it will crumble. Served as is, this is a great tasting meat loaf. If you wish you can also top it with a tomato cream sauce (see page 149.)
Serves 4 for 40 cents each, 50 cents each with sauce.

Variations: If you have leftover pizza, use it in place of 1/2 of the meat. Grind the pizza in a food processor or just mince it into small pieces by hand. Omit thyme.
Give your meat loaf a southwestern touch by adding 1/2 cup of salsa. Omit thyme. Use crushed tortilla chips instead of bread crumbs. Serve with fresh slices of avocado or a salad with guacamole dressing.

To make bread crumbs, chop two slices of bread into cubes, then crumb them at high speed in a blender. Makes 3/4 cup.

Southern Fried Chicken

1 fryer, cut up
8 strips of bacon
1 cup flour seasoned with 1 tsp. red pepper
1/2 cup milk mixed with 1 beaten egg

Fry bacon in skillet. Remove and drain. Dip chicken pieces into milk and egg mix, coating them well, then dredge them in flour. Let sit at least 30 minutes. Add enough oil to bacon fat to bring oil up to 1/2 inch. Heat to 350°, then add chicken. Once browned, cover and reduce heat, cooking for 20 to 25 minutes, turning occasionally, until the chicken is golden brown. Drain on paper towels; keep warm. Garnish chicken with bacon; serve with cream gravy. Satisfies 4 at 80 cents apiece.

Cream Gravy: Pour off all but 1/4 cup of the pan drippings. Add 2 tablespoons flour, stirring. Gradually add 2 cups of half and half, stirring until thickened.

If you have leftovers, carefully cut them into julienned strips that preserve the breaded skin as well as the meat. Put on top of a bed of lettuce and add some hard-cooked egg quarters, crumbled bacon, avocado slices, grated colby cheese, and a honey mustard dressing, and you have a fried chicken salad.

Honey Mustard Dressing: Mix in a blender 1/4 cup honey, 2 tablespoons salad oil, 3 tablespoons white wine vinegar, 1/4 cup coarse Dijon mustard, and a splash of Tabasco sauce. Cost: 4 cents an ounce.

Roasted Chicken

1 fryer
3 cups grated sweet apples
1/3 cup raisins
1/4 cup minced celery
2 tbsp. grated almonds
1 1/2 tbsp. each minced onion and chopped parsley
1 tbsp. fresh lemon juice
1/4 tsp. each cinnamon and nutmeg
5 onions, cut in half
8 small creamer potatoes, unpeeled
4 carrots, quartered and cut into 2-inch segments

Remove innards, if any. Drain chicken and pat dry. Rub inside and out with olive oil. To make stuffing, combine fruits, almonds, celery, onion, parsley, lemon juice,and seasonings. Stuff dressing into inner cavity of chicken. Close with skewers or pins. Place chicken in buttered roasting pan and surround with 1/2 chopped onion. Roast at 450° for 15 minutes. Add to the pan 2 cups of chicken stock and 2 teaspoons fresh grated lemon peel. Add to stock carrots, onions, and potatoes. Lower heat to 325° and roast 45 minutes. Remove cover and roast chicken 15 minutes longer.

Remove chicken and vegetables to serving platters. Add 1/2 tablespoon of arrowroot to pan juices; cook until blended. Add 1/3 cup red wine. Serve sauce in gravy bowl.

Makes 4 servings at 90 cents a person with leftovers for salads, fill-ups, etc.

Bud Beef

1 3/4 lbs. boneless chuck, cubed
2 tbsp. each butter and oil
2 large onions
1 tsp. crushed garlic
2 tbsp. flour
2 cups of beer
pinch of thyme, sugar, and nutmeg
1/2 loaf of French bread
3 tbsp. coarse Dijon mustard

Sauté beef in foaming oil and butter. Add onions and garlic; cook until soft. Sprinkle on flour, stirring until flour absorbs the fat. Transfer meat to a casserole and add beer and seasonings. Bake 2 hours in a 350° oven. Slice French bread thickly, then spread one side of each slice with mustard. Place slices mustard side down on top of beef; return to oven without a lid for a final 20 minutes, until bread is browned. Serve with a salad and more French bread.   Serves 4 at $1.15 cents each.

Dinner Menu

Beef Brisket
Lyonnaise Potatoes
Bric-a-Broc
Oatmeal Muffins
Hot Tea
Fresh Fruit and Sugar Cookies
Cost: $1.45 a person

Frontera Pork Chops

4 pork chops (or 4 boneless pork medallions)
2 tbsp. butter
2 green onions, chopped
1/2 lb. mushrooms, quartered
paprika to taste
1 tbsp. flour
1/4 cup dry sherry
1/2 cup chicken broth
1/8 cup heavy cream

Sauté pork in butter. Add onions and mushrooms; cook until soft. Sprinkle with paprika and flour, stirring until flour is absorbed. Add sherry and broth. Stir until well blended. Cover and cook over low heat for 35 to 45 minutes, depending on thickness of pork slices. Stir in cream and bring to a boil over high heat. Reduce cream sauce until thick and smooth.

Makes four servings at 80 cents each.

Sherry comes from Jerez de la Frontera in Spain, hence the name of this dish. Served with sweet potatoes, Majorcan peas, and hot tea, this is one of my wife's favorite meals–and the total cost can be as little as $1.05 a serving! That means that if you have the room in your budget, you can easily make the pork slices a little bit thicker–and still stay beneath the magic mark of $1.98 for dinner!

On the other hand, you can serve the same dish with only 3 ounces of pork apiece, by cutting the slices into strips, fixing it as above, and then serving the dish as the topping for the sweet potato. This would reduce the cost to only 90 cents for the complete dinner.

1/2 lb. spaghetti noodles, homemade or commercial
2/3 lb. bulk Italian sausage
2 cups tomato cream sauce

Cook spaghetti according to directions on package. (It is not necessary to salt the water.) Meanwhile, sauté crumbled sausage over low heat until thoroughly cooked. Add tomato cream sauce to sausage; blend thoroughly and cook for 5 to 10 minutes. Drain spaghetti and pile on serving plates. Top with sauce. Serve with freshly grated Parmesan cheese.

Serves 4 at 70 cents each. Add a salad and a crusty loaf of Italian bread (with or without garlic and cheese) for a complete meal at 89 cents each.

Variations:

Spaghetti Carbonara: Fry 4 slices of bacon until crisp. Remove bacon and drain. Sauté 1 chopped onion in bacon drippings; set aside. Combine three beaten eggs with 2 ounces grated Parmesan cheese, and 3 chopped sprigs of parsley. Add cooked spaghetti to cheese and egg mixture; toss quickly. Add onions, drippings, and crumbled bacon. Toss and serve.

Cost: 20 cents a serving.

Zucchini Spaghetti: Sauté a sliced zucchini in 2 tablespoons olive oil. Add 1 tablespoon basil, a dash of pepper, and 1 teaspoon garlic flakes; toss lightly. Mix drained spaghetti with 1 tablespoon each grated Parmesan cheese and butter. Quickly stir in 1 beaten egg. Toss with zucchini. Sprinkle with more Parmesan cheese and serve. Cost: 15 cents a serving.

Lasagna

3/4 lb. lasagna noodles, homemade or commercial
1/2 lb. each bulk Italian sausage and ground beef
3 tbsp. butter
3/4 lb. sliced mozzarella cheese
3/4 lb. ricotta cheese
3 cups tomato cream sauce

Cook lasagna as directed. Drain. Sauté crumbled meat in 3 tablespoons butter. Oil a straight-side baking dish. Place one layer of lasagna on the bottom. Cover with a layer of the mixed meats, followed by a layer of sauce, a layer of mozzarella, and a layer of ricotta. Repeat layering in this way until all ingredients except one-half the sauce has been used. Sprinkle with Parmesan and top with remaining sauce. Bake at 400° for 45 minutes. Serves 6 at $1.15 each.

Cannelloni

1/2 pound flat homemade pasta, cut in 4" squares
1/2 pound bulk Italian sausage, crumbled
1 pkg. frozen chopped spinach
1/2 pound ricotta cheese
Parmesan cheese
2 cups tomato cream sauce

Sauté sausage on low. Cook spinach 6 minutes; drain. Spread ricotta cheese over each 4" square of pasta. Top with sausage, then spinach. Sprinkle with grated Parmesan. Roll up; arrange in dish. Top with sauce. Bake 20 minutes at 375°. Serves 4 at 85 cents each.

1/2 lb. boneless sirloin steak
1 tbsp. each butter and oil
4 chopped green onions
1 cup sliced fresh mushrooms
1 tbsp. flour
1/2 cup beef stock or red wine
1/2 tsp. Worcestershire
1/2 cup sour cream
4 large baking potatoes

Bake potatoes at 400° for 1 hour. Cut steak into thin strips, one inch long. Sauté in butter and oil until brown, then add onions and mushrooms. Remove meat and vegetables to a plate; add flour, stirring until frothy. Blend in stock or Worcestershire sauce. Return beef and vegetables to pan, heat through. Remove from heat, blend in sour cream at once. Serve on top of the baked potatoes, which have been split and opened.

Serves four at 45 cents apiece.

Dinner Menu

Meat Loaf of the Gods
Potato Pancakes
Southern Squash
Blueberry Squares
Hot Tea
Icebox Pudding
Cost: $1.30

Veal Francaise On Top

1/2 lb. cubed veal steaks
2 tbsp. butter and 1 tbsp. oil
1 cup sliced mushrooms
1/2 cup sliced asparagus tips (save stalks)
2 tbsp. cognac
1/3 cup heavy cream
4 large baking potatoes

Bake potatoes at 400° for 1 hour. Cut veal in thin strips 1 inch long. Sauté in butter and oil; add mushrooms and asparagus tips. Add cognac and flame briefly in pan. Add cream; cook about 5 minutes. Serve on top of the potatoes, which have been split and opened.
    Serves 4 at $1.20 each.

Seafood Cream on Top

3/4 lb. assorted seafood–shrimp, scallops, etc.
1/2 cup heavy cream
2 leeks, julienned in thin strips
4 tbsp. butter
white wine
4 large baking potatoes

Bake potatoes at 400° for 1 hour. Sauté leeks in 2 tbsp. butter for 2 minutes. Add a splash of white wine. Simmer 2 minutes. Add cream; simmer two minutes. Cook seafood quickly in microwave. Add to sauce. Swirl in rest of butter. Serve on top of potatoes.
    Serves 4 at $1.20 each.

1/2 lb. cooked ham cubes
1/2 lb. fresh asparagus
2 green onions, chopped
2 tbsp. butter
1 1/2 tbsp. flour
1 cup half and half
Dijon mustard
4 large baking potatoes

Bake potatoes at 400° for 1 hour. Snap asparagus stalks in half, storing the bottom halves for other uses. Slice the tip ends diagonally; sauté with onion for 3 or 4 minutes in butter. Remove asparagus. Add flour to melted butter over low heat. Add half and half slowly, stirring. As it thickens, add a tablespoon or so of mustard, to taste, stirring until completely blended. Add ham and asparagus. Heat through. If sauce is too thick, thin with more half and half. If too thin, thicken by stirring in a sprinkling of arrowroot.

Serves 4 at 75 cents each.

Variations:

Madeira Ham on Top: Omit asparagus and onions and increase ham to 3/4 lb. In addition to Dijon mustard, swirl 1 tablespoon of Madeira wine into the sauce. Reduces cost by 15 cents a serving.

Spinach Ham on Top: Replace asparagus with a half package of cooked frozen chopped spinach and one small can of artichoke hearts, chopped. Finish sauce with a splash of Tabasco. Garnish with grated Parmesan cheese.

Paella

2 tbsp. olive oil
2 cloves of garlic, minced
1/2 cup chopped onions
1 Italian or Spanish sausage, cut in slices
1 cup rice
2 cups chicken broth
1 cup cooked chicken strips
1/4 tsp. tumeric (saffron if you have it)
1 package frozen peas
1 cup raw shrimp, peeled and deveined
1 cup chopped cooked ham

Sauté garlic and onion in olive oil in a wok, paella pan, or large skillet. Add sausage; cook 3 to 5 minutes. Add 1 cup rice, 2 cups broth, chicken, ham, and tumeric. Boil, reduce heat, and simmer 15 minutes. Add peas and shrimp. Mix thoroughly. Cook another 5 minutes, then serve. It's a whole meal in itself.
Makes 4 servings for 75 cents each.

Depending upon your budget and tastes, paella can be expanded to include clams, mussels, scallops, and calamari. Keep an eye peeled for when these items—or others you may prefer—are available at sale prices.

Surf & Turf on a Skewer

Steak! Shrimp! Grilled! Here's how to do it inexpensively.

1/2 pound sirloin steak, cut in small cubes
24 raw medium shrimp
12 slices bacon
1 cup fresh pineapple chunks
1/2 cup soy sauce
1/3 cup dry sherry
1/4 cup vegetable oil
1/4 cup sugar
2 cloves garlic, minced
1 tsp. ground ginger

Swirl soy sauce, sherry, oil, sugar, garlic, and ginger together. Let stand 1 hour to blend flavors. Marinate meat and shrimp for at least 1 hour in sauce. Cut bacon in half. Place cubed meat, shrimp, bacon, and pineapple chunks on skewers until all ingredients are used up. Brush with marinade, then grill over moderate heat on a charcoal grill or bistro-style grill. Cook until shrimp turn pink in color and bacon is done. Serve on rice.

Serves 4 at 95 cents each.

You might want to precook the bacon lightly, so that it will be thoroughly cooked when the rest of the items are ready. Also, cut the steak so that you end up with as many pieces of it as shrimp and bacon (24 each).

Fish and Chips

1 1/2 lbs. filet of flounder or cod
1 1/2 lbs. potatoes, julienned for fries
1 1/2 cups flour
1 tsp. salt
1/4 tsp. pepper
1 tbsp. melted butter
2 eggs, separated
3/4 cup flat beer

Beat egg yolks. Blend in flour, salt, pepper, and butter. Stir in beer. Refrigerate batter 3 to 12 hours. Fold in stiffly beaten egg whites. Soak potato juliennes in cold water 30 minutes; dry thoroughly. Fry in oil at 375° until golden brown; drain and keep warm. Cut fish into serving pieces; dip in batter, then deep fry in oil until golden brown. Serves 4 at $1.10 each.

The same batter can be used to make chicken and chips, using small pieces of white meat that result from deboning breasts.

Pork Roast

1 butterflied pork rib roast (4 lb.)
1/3 cup each dried apricots, prunes, & applesauce

Untie roast and roll out. Lay chopped apricots, prunes, and apple in the crease of the roast. Roll back up; tie; and bake in a 350° oven for 2 hours, or until a meat thermometer registers 185.

Makes 12 servings at 85 cents each.

Cantonese Stir Fry

1/2 lb. shelled medium shrimp
1/2 lb. chicken livers
2 cups broccoli, cut in small florets
2 green onions, chopped
1/4 cup oil
1 1/2 tbsp. soy sauce
1 tsp. ginger
1 tsp. sugar
2 tbsp. sherry

Parboil broccoli for 3 minutes; drain. Cut each liver into quarters. Sprinkle the shrimp and livers with a table-spoon each of oil. Heat remaining oil in a wok or large skillet. Add livers, shrimp, and onions. Sprinkle with ginger and soy sauce. Stir fry for 90 seconds. Add broccoli, sugar, and sherry. Stir fry for 2 minutes.

Serves 4 at 78 cents each.

Dinner Menu

Daube
Rice Pilaf
Spinach Soufflé
French Bread
Hot Tea
Chocolate Waffle Sundae

Cost: $1.15 a person

Sludge

1 pound ground meat–beef, turkey, pork, etc.
2 tbsp. margarine or butter
3 chopped green onions
1/2 cup chopped green pepper and carrot
1 can tomatoes
8 ounces uncooked macaroni or pasta
1 cup grated cheese

Sauté meat in butter; add onions, peppers, and carrots. Add tomatoes and then the uncooked macaroni. Add 2 cups of water or vegetable broth–or part water and part red wine. Bring to boil, then reduce the heat and simmer for 15 to 20 minutes. Add more liquid if needed. Stir in grated cheese and serve.
Serves 4 for 85 cents each.

Variations: There are as many variations on sludge as your imagination can conjure. The most obvious way to vary this dish is by using different kinds of cheeses and meats. Or, instead of green pepper or carrot, throw in an equivalent amount of julienned turnip and celery.

Nassi Goreng

3 cups cooked rice, cold
2 medium onions, chopped fine
2 cloves garlic, minced
1 tsp. chili powder
1/2 lb. cooked pork or ham
4 eggs, beaten with 1/4 cup milk
butter

Sauté onions and garlic in 2 tablespoons butter. Add rice and chili powder, blending thoroughly. Add ham and let cook on low heat several minutes. In a separate pan, melt remaining butter. Pour eggs and milk mixture into pan; cook quickly to make one large omelet. Slice omelet in strips. Ladle rice into serving bowls or plates; top each serving with omelet strips. Serve with traditional Indonesian side dishes such as chutney, peanuts, coconut, sambal oelek, and baked bananas.

Serves 4 at 50 cents each.

Homemade Sambal Oelek: Mix 2 tablespoons finely chopped red chili peppers with 1/2 tablespoon oil, 1/2 teaspoon salt, 1/2 teaspoon lemon juice, and 1/2 teaspoon grated lemon rind, forming a paste. Store in the refrigerator in a tightly-covered jar.

Turkey Tetrazzini

1 1/2 cups cooked pieces of turkey
4 oz. macaroni or spaghetti
1/4 lb. sliced mushrooms
1 1/2 tbsp. butter
1 tbsp. flour
1 cup turkey or chicken broth
Parmesan cheese
1/2 cup heavy cream
2 tbsp. dry white wine

Cook the pasta; drain well. Sauté the mushrooms in 2 tablespoons butter. Combine with pasta. Blend together butter, flour, and broth, cooking gently. Remove from heat and stir in cream and wine. Place macaroni or spaghetti in a greased baking dish, creating a cavity in the center of the noodles. Fill it with turkey, then pour sauce all around the top of the noodles and turkey. Top with grated Parmesan cheese. Bake at 375° until top is bubbly and lightly browned. Serves 4 at 40 cents each.

Variations: Use chicken or tuna instead of turkey. Or add 1 cup of broccoli florets and make it a quick and easy turkey divan. Top with a layer of mozzarella cheese. Add: 10 cents per serving.

O Sole Mio

1/2 cup dried bread crumbs
6 tbsp. butter
1 tbsp. chopped parsley
1 cup cooked, chopped shrimp
1 egg, beaten
nutmeg
4 small filets of sole

Combine bread crumbs, butter, parsley, shrimp, nutmeg, and egg. Spread a thin layer of this mixture on top of each filet of sole, patting it lightly so that it stays in place. Place fish in buttered baking dish and bake at 350° for 20 minutes.
Serves 4 at $1.45 each.

It is not necessary to use sole in this recipe; flounder, halibut, turbot, and sole can all be used interchangeably. Use the one that is the best value.

This same recipe can be made without the shrimp. Dip each filet in the beaten egg, then roll it lightly in the bread crumbs, which have been mixed with the parsley and nutmeg. Sauté in butter (use only half as much) until done, two or three minutes per side.
This approach reduces cost to $1.30 a serving.
Almost any fllet of fish can be cooked using this method.

Rouladen

1 onion, diced
4 round steaks, cut or pounded very thin
1/4 tsp. rosemary
1/2 pickle
2 oz. salt pork or bacon
2 tbsp. butter or oil
1/3 cup flour
2 tbsp. paprika
1 clove garlic
1/4 tsp. each thyme & marjoram
2 cups beef broth
1 cup tomato purée
1 cup red wine

Sprinkle rosemary and half of the diced onion on the steaks, along with the pickle and salt pork, both chopped. Roll steak and secure each roll with toothpicks. Brown steaks in butter; remove to casserole. Sauté remaining onion, then add flour, paprika, garlic, thyme, and marjoram, mixing well. Add beef broth, stirring to mix evenly with the roux (the flour, butter, and seasoning combination); add tomato purée and bring to a boil. Pour sauce over steaks, cover, and bake at 350° for 2 hours. Add red wine 10 minutes before meat finishes cooking.

Serves 4 at 60 cents each.

Shrimp Curry

1 minced onion
2 slices of bacon, chopped
1/4 cup curry powder
1 tbsp. flour
1 apple, chopped
2 tbsp. lemon juice
1 tbsp. tomato paste
1 tbsp. honey
2 cups vegetable or chicken broth
1/2 cup fruit preserves
3/4 lb. cooked shrimp, peeled and deveined

Sauté onion and bacon in bacon fat until onion is golden. Add curry, cook briefly, then add flour. Add everything else except the shrimp, cover, and simmer for 30 minutes. Purée for 2 or 3 seconds only in the blender. Add shrimp and serve on rice with at least 3 or 4 of the usual accompaniments for curries: raisins, chutney, chopped peanuts, coconut, banana slices, and chopped hard-cooked eggs.
    Serves 4 at $1.05 a serving.

Variations: Replace the shrimp with–
3/4 cup cooked chicken. Saves 70 cents a serving
3/4 cup cooked pork or ham. Saves 50 cents.
3/4 cup cooked lamb. Saves 50 a serving.
8 hard-cooked eggs, quartered. Saves 60 cents.

Chicken Fried Steak

4 round steaks, cut very thin or pounded
1/2 cup milk mixed with 1 beaten egg
1 cup flour seasoned with nutmeg
butter

Dip steaks in egg mixture, then in flour. Slowly brown meat in hot butter, turning once. Simmer for 45 minutes to an hour until tender. Serve with cream gravy (optional) as described on page 78.
Serves 4 at 80 cents each.

Steak and Lentils

3/4 lb. flank steak, cut in thin strips
2 green onions, chopped
3 tbsp. finely chopped chives
1/4 cup brandy
1 tbsp. Worcestershire sauce
1 cup dried lentils
1/2 cup beef stock

Sauté steak, onions, and chives briefly in 2 tbsp. butter. Flame with brandy, then add Worcestershire. Lower heat and add lentils and stock. Cook, stirring occasionally, for about 20 minutes.
Serves 4 at 80 cents each.

Lentils are usually found in soups and stews. Here, they lend a nutty texture and flavor that makes this a hearty meal, indeed.

Cabbage Rolls

1 head green cabbage
1 lb. ground meat–beef, turkey, veal, lamb, or pork
1/4 cup each chopped onions, green pepper & celery
1 tbsp. Worcestershire sauce
3/4 cup cooked rice or lentils
2 tbsp. currants (or raisins)
1 can tomato paste (6 oz.)
1 can tomatoes (10 oz.)
1/4 cup heavy cream
splash of Tabasco

Carefully remove 8 outer leaves from the head of cabbage, being sure not to break them. Cook 5 minutes in boiling water. Drain and set aside. Save rest of cabbage for other uses. Combine meat, chopped vegetables, rice, currants, and Worcestershire. Mix well. Place equal amounts of this mixture in the center of each cabbage leaf. Fold in end flaps first, then roll up to form a cylinder. Place seam side down in a buttered baking dish. Combine tomato paste with crushed tomatoes. Cook briefly, then add cream and the splash of Tabasco. Heat until sauce begins to thicken slightly. Pour sauce over cabbage rolls; bake at 350° for 1 hour.
   Serves 4 at 50 cents each.

Variation: If you use grape leaves, you can call this dish "dolmas" like the Greeks do.

Dutch Kale

1 lb. Dutch beef sausage
3 lb. kale
3 pounds boiling potatoes, quartered
1/4 cup butter
milk
8 miniature sweet gherkins

Wash the kale, shred it into strips, and boil for 40 minutes in 1 cup of water. Add potatoes and sausage. Simmer 30 minutes. If needed, add more liquid. Remove sausage. Mash potatoes and kale, adding butter and milk as needed. Serve equal portions of sausage with equal portions of potato and kale.

Serves 4 at 95 cents each.

This traditional Dutch winter dish is usually served with miniature sweet pickles. Each diner cuts up the sausage and pickle and blends it with the kale-potato mixture to suit his or her own style and taste.

Sateh Bami

1 lb. pork, cut in cubes
4 tbsp. peanut butter
1 tbsp. soy sauce
3 tbsp. catsup
2 tsp. molasses or honey

Mix peanut butter with 8 tablespoons hot water, the soy sauce, catsup, and molasses or honey. Simmer for 5 minutes, then cool. Marinate pork cubes in sauce for at least 24 hours, refrigerated. (Meat and sauce can be frozen at this point, if you're making more than you need for one meal.) Put pork on skewers and barbecue over moderate heat on a charcoal or bistro grill.
Serves 4 at 30 cents each.

T-Bone Bonus

4 T-bone steaks, cut only 1/4 inch thick
2 onions, sliced thickly, brushed with olive oil
1/2 oz. crumbled blue cheese
2 tbsp. butter, at room temperature
1 tsp. fresh garlic chips
a dash of Tabasco

Combine blue cheese, butter, garlic, and Tabasco. Shape into a bar. Wrap in wax paper and refrigerate. Brush onions with olive oil; grill 3 minutes on each side. Place steaks on grill; as thin as these are, they will cook very quickly. Serve steaks with a slab of blue cheese butter on each and the grilled onions. Serves 4 at $1.45 each.

Daube

3 lbs. lean beef stew meat or chuck, cut in cubes
3 onions, coarsely chopped
5 cloves of garlic
bits of salt pork (or two chopped strips of bacon)
1/2 tsp. each thyme and summer savory
orange peel
1 clove

Place ingredients in a little water and add a glass and a half of red wine. Cover and bake at 325° for 4 hours.
Makes 8 to 10 servings at 55 cents each.

Mary's Lamb

1 lamb roast, about 5 pounds
2 tbsp. chopped fresh rosemary, or 2 tsp. dried
1 lemon peel, grated
1 tsp. fresh black pepper
1/2 tsp. dried thyme
1/4 tsp. ground allspice
2 large cloves of garlic, chopped

Combine herbs and rub mixture over whole surface of the lamb roast. Refrigerate for 2 to 12 hours Then roast at 500° for 10 minutes; reduce heat to 325°. Baste two or three times while cooking. Roast a total of 2 hours, or until inner temperature of roast reaches 165 degrees.
Serves 16 at 90 cents each.

Shrimp Stir Fry

3/4 lb. medium shrimp
4 green onions, chopped diagonally
1/4 head of cabbage, shredded
1 pkg. frozen peas
1/4 lb. snow peas or sugar peas
1 carrot, cut in paper thin strips with a peeler
1 parsnip, cut in paper thin strips
2 tbsp. oil
1 tbsp. soy sauce
Chinese 5-spice powder

Peel and devein shrimp. Sauté onions in foaming oil in a wok (or skillet). Add carrot and parsnip, plus soy sauce and spices. Add fresh snow peas, cooking lightly, and then frozen peas and shredded cabbage. Cover and cook two minutes; stirring regularly. Add shrimp and cook until they turn pink and white.

Serves 4 at 80 cents each.

Variations: Substitute any kind of seafood or thinly sliced meat for the shrimp: pork, beef, chicken, turkey, bay scallops, crab, or lobster. You can also create a variety of effects by changing the seasonings from Chinese to Italian (olive oil, garlic, and oregano), Mexican (salsa, jalapeño peppers, and cumin), and so on.

Veal Oscar Stir Fry: Use imitation or real crab meat, ground veal, asparagus tips, and 2 tablespoons of hollandaise sauce. Eliminate peas, snow peas, parsnip, and soy sauce.

Lobster & Shrimp Soufflé

1 small Brazilian lobster tail (3 oz.)
1/3 lb. medium shrimp
3 tbsp. butter
3 tbsp. flour
1 cup half and half
nutmeg
3 egg yolks, beaten
1/3 cup grated Swiss cheese
3 egg whites, whipped until stiff

Remove lobster and shrimp meat from shells; chop into little pieces. Sauté quickly in 1 tbsp. butter, until the meat turns white. Set aside. Reduce pan juices in half; add 2 tablespoons heavy cream and 1 tablespoon brandy. Stir until thickened, then set aside. Melt butter over low heat. Stir in flour, cooking for 5 minutes. Add half and half slowly. Stir until thickened and smooth. Add in cooked seafood. When heated, remove pan from stove and stir in 3 beaten egg yolks. Season with nut-meg. Blend in grated cheese and let cool. Fold in stiff egg whites. Pour mixture into a buttered and lightly floured soufflé dish. Bake at 400° for 18 to 20 minutes, or until the soufflé is puffed and golden brown. Serve with reserved sauce (reheat in microwave just before serving).
   Serves 4 elegantly for $1.50 each.

   If your local market carries frozen langostino meat, you may be able to use it in place of the lobster for a lot less. You can also save by eliminating the lobster and increasing the cheese to 2/3 cup. A small filet of fresh tuna or salmon can also be used triumphantly.

Catfish Curry

4 catfish filets
2 tbsp. butter
2 chopped green onions
1/2 tsp. curry powder
1/2 tbsp. cracked pepper
1 tbsp. lemon juice
1/2 cup heavy cream

Sauté fish and onions over medium heat in butter, curry, and pepper. Cook 3 to 5 minutes; remove fish. Add lemon juice and cream; cook over high heat until cream is reduced. Return fish to pan; heat and serve.
Serves 4 at 75 cents each.

Chicken Veronica

2 whole chicken breasts (4 half-breasts)
2 tbsp. butter
2 tbsp. dry white wine
1/4 tsp. each tarragon and basil
1/2 cup heavy cream
1/2 cup seedless green grapes

Remove skin and bone from chicken breasts, saving for stockpot. Sauté breasts in butter until golden on both sides. Add wine and herbs. Cover and simmer for 5 minutes. Remove chicken. Reduce pan juices to syrup; add cream. Boil until thickened. Stir grapes into cream; return breasts to pan to reheat.
Serves 4 at 90 cents each.

Vegetables

One of the the easiest ways to save money and stretch the food budget is to learn how to prepare fresh vegetables. Fresh vegetables are amazingly inexpensive–and chock full of the nutrition, fiber, and vitamins that we need.

There are, of course, people who do not like vegetables. I disliked parsnips, turnips, and eggplant when I was a kid. But I quickly outgrew these dislikes, once I learned how to fix them correctly. I am willing to make a bet. If you dislike a vegetable, you are probably not cooking it properly. Learn to cook vegetables correctly, and it will be love at first bite.

Whenever possible, buy and prepare fresh vegetables. Canning changes the taste–and not for the better. It also robs vegetables of much of their nutrition. Frozen vegetables survive better and are a great convenience, but you pay for it–especially if it is highly processed, as in a stir fry combination. You can buy a frozen package of "stir fry" vegetables at the grocery for $1.39. Or you can make an equivalent amount for 52 cents.

Baked Potatoes

4 medium baking potatoes
bacon fat

Wash and dry the potatoes. Rub bacon fat all over the skin. Pierce the skin with a fork. Bake the potatoes at 400 for 1 hour. Serve with butter or sour cream or both, chopped chives, crumbled bacon, or grated cheddar cheese.

Cost per serving: 15 cents (toppings are extra).

Baked Stuffed Potatoes: Take four baked potatoes and carefully cut an ellipse lengthwise along the top of each. Set the top aside and carefully scoop out the potato pulp, taking care not to break the skin at any point. Mash the pulp with 3 tablespoons butter and 2 tablespoons half and half. When potatoes have reached the proper consistency, spoon the mashed pulp back into the shells. Return the potatoes to a 400° oven for 10 to 15 minutes. If necessary, run them under the broiler just before serving, until the tops are browned.

Serves 4 at 20 cents each.

And don't throw away the leftover skins. Save them (in the freezer) until you have a dozen or so. Butter them and sprinkle them with grated cheese, then run them under a broiler quickly for a tasty, crunchy appetizer costing 1 cent a serving.

Variations on baked stuffed potatoes:
Add 1/4 cup grated cheese while mashing potatoes.
Add crumbled bacon while mashing potatoes.
Add 1/4 cup sour cream while mashing potatoes.

Boiled Potatoes

4 medium red, white, or creamer potatoes

Place potatoes in a pot, cover with water, and bring to a boil. Boil slowly for 30 minutes. Drain and serve as is, with butter on the side. Or roll the potatoes in Cajun or Mexican seasonings. Or roll them in melted butter blended with chopped parsley or chives.
Serves 4 at 12 cents each.

Mashed potatoes: If appearance matters, peel the potatoes before boiling. Otherwise, leave the peels on. Mash 4 cooked potatoes with a fork or potato masher-or run them through a blender or food processer. Add 2 tablespoons butter, 1/2 teaspoon salt (if desired), and 1/3 cup hot milk or cream. Whip until creamy but not runny. Serves 4 at 15 cents each.

Variations: Add 1/4 cup grated cheese with the hot milk.
Add chopped parsley or bacon with the hot milk.

Chantilly Potatoes: Add 1/2 cup grated cheese to 1/2 cup heavy cream that has been whipped until stiff. Mound up cooked mashed potatoes in an ovenproof dish; press in center to create a crater. Fill crater with chantilly mixture; bake in oven until cheese is melted and the potatoes are beginning to brown.

Lyonnaise Potatoes: Sauté two chopped onions in 4 tablespoons butter. Slice and dice 4 small boiled potatoes; add to onions. Cook 5 to 10 minutes until lightly browned. Serves 4 for 18 cents each.

Potatoes Anna

2 large potatoes
3 tbsp. butter and oil
1/2 grated onion
Parmesan cheese

Slice potatoes very thin. Dry slices on paper towels. Heat butter and oil in a large skillet or on a griddle. Arrange potato slices in an overlapping ring around the outer edge of the pan. Add other overlapping circles in the center of the ring, until slices are used up. Sprinkle potatoes with onion and cheese. If necessary, add a second layer. Place a round cake pan on top of the potatoes and set a heavy object, like a can or pot of water, in the center of the cake pan. Sauté potatoes until underside is golden brown–about 20 minutes. Remove weight and plate. Carefully turn entire mass of potatoes at once. Cook until browned on the underside as well. Cut in quarters and serve, drizzling each serving with any butter remaining in pan.
Serves 4 at 18 cents each.

Dinner Menu

Chicken Veronica
Potatoes Anna
Creole Lima Beans
Hot Tea
Coconut Mousse Pie
Cost: $1.85

Potato Pancakes

2 cups grated potatoes
3 eggs, beaten
1 1/2 tbsps. flour
2 tbsp. grated onion and 1 tsp. chives
1/2 cup applesauce

Combine all ingredients, mixing thoroughly. Shape into patties 3 inches in diameter and 1/8 inch high. Fry in butter and oil on a griddle or in a frying pan.
    Serves 4 at 20 cents each.

Unfries

4 medium potatoes
1/4 cup bacon fat
salt or paprika

Cut the potatoes in julienned strips to suit your tastes. Soak them in cold water 10 minutes, then drain them between towels. Spread in a single layer in a flat oven safe dish. Pour the melted bacon fat over them, and stir them until coated. Bake at 450° for 30 to 40 minutes, turning the fries several times. Drain on paper towels. Sprinkle with salt or paprika or both, to taste.
    Serves 4 at 10 cents each.

    Why spend 20 to 30 cents a serving to buy frozen fries in the store, when you can make them yourself for so much less?   In one year, you could save $350 on potatoes alone, by fixing them from scratch.

Sweet Potato Puffs

2 cups cooked, mashed sweet potatoes (yams)
1 large banana, mashed or 1 cup apple sauce
3 tbsp. butter
3/4 cup half and half
2 eggs, separated
nutmeg
brown sugar

Blend together everything except the eggs. When smooth, blend in egg yolks. Whip egg whites until stiff, then fold into sweet potato mixture. Pour into buttered casserole. Bake at 375° for 30 minutes.
Serves 4 at 30 cents each.

Yammies

4 medium sweet potatoes or yams
bacon fat
1/4 cup butter
2 tbsp. brown sugar
1/4 cup walnuts or pecans
dash of nutmeg
a splash of Southern Comfort

Scrub potatoes, leaving skin intact. Rub with bacon fat. Cut small slice from end of potato. Pierce potatoes with fork several times. Bake at 400° for 1 hour. When done, slice top of potato and serve with yammy sauce made by mixing last 5 ingredients and heating lightly.
Serves 4 at 40 cents each.

Rice Pilaf

You can always cook rice the way they tell you to on the package. You will end up with nice rice. But why not end up with a great rice? Try this simple recipe:

1 cup rice
2 tbsp. butter
1/2 cup fInely chopped onion
2 cups chicken or vegetable broth

Sauté onion in butter in a large skillet. Add rice, cooking until golden and translucent. Do not brown. Add stock and bring to a boil. Cover and cook for 25 minutes, until all moisture is absorbed.
Serves 4 at 8 cents each.

Variations:
Adding raisins and peanuts is a good way to serve this rice with a curry.
Add 1/2 cup cooked lentils.
Add a dash or two of Tabasco sauce for a fiery rice.

Chinese Asparagus

1 lb. asparagus
3 tbsp. butter

Snap stems; save woody ends for other uses (see page 117). Slice tip ends very thinly, on a diagonal. Sauté in butter for 3 minutes, stirring briskly. Cover and simmer on low heat another minute. Serves 4 for 16 cents each.

Bric-a-Broc

1 beaten egg
1 10-ounce package of frozen broccoli, thawed
1 8.5 ounce can of creamed corn
1 cup herb stuffing mix
3 tbsp. butter or margarine
1 tbsp. chopped green onion

Combine egg, broccoli, corn, and onion in a bowl. In a separate saucepan, melt butter, then add the stuffing, tossing to coat. Stir buttered stuffing into vegetable mixture; turn into an ungreased one-quart casserole. Sprinkle with extra stuffing. Bake uncovered at 350° for 40 minutes. Serves 6 at 14 cents each.

Carrots & Leeks

3 carrots, scraped
1 large leek, cleaned
2 tbsp. butter or margarine
2 ounces heavy cream

Cut the carrots into matchstick-sized pieces. Sauté in butter on low heat for 10 minutes. Chop off most of the green tops of the leeks; reserve for vegetable stock or soup. Cut rest of leek into julienned strips the same size as the carrot matchsticks. Add to carrots; sauté on low heat another five to ten minutes. Add cream; turn heat to high. Cook until cream is reduced by half–one or two minutes. If desired, add a sprinkling of mace.
Serves 4 at 16 cents each.

Corn on the Cob

8 ears fresh corn on the cob

Bring a large pot of water to boil. Remove husks and silk from each ear. Plunge corn into water; return to boil, then take pot off the heat. Let corn sit in water 10 to 20 minutes. Serve with plenty of butter.
Serves 4 for 24 cents each.

Bacorn Pie

3 strips bacon
1 cup bread crumbs
1 cup sliced tomatoes
1/2 cup sliced green peppers
2 tbsp. butter
2 cups uncooked corn

Lay bacon in bottom of baking dish. Fill dish with other ingredients, making sure the top layer is corn. Top with more bread crumbs and dot with butter. Bake at 350° for 40 minutes, or until done. To serve, grate fresh cheese over the top.
Serves 4 at 18 cents each.

Grilled Tomatoes

4 ripe tomatoes
3 tbsp. olive oil
1 tbsp. red wine vinegar
1 tsp. Dijon mustard
2 tbsp. basil

Slice tomatoes 1/2 inch thick. Marinate for 30 minutes in remaining ingredients. Set carefully on moderate hot charcoal grill. Cook for several minutes, then turn and cook the second side.
    Serves 4 at 22 cents each.

    Variations: You can grill just about any vegetable you can slice. Just brush them with oil and grill them over a moderate fire for a few minutes. Try it with zucchini, carrots, peppers, onions, and corn.

Fried Green Tomatoes

4 green tomatoes
1 cup cornmeal
bacon drippings

Slice tomatoes 1/4-inch thick. Dredge in cornmeal, then sauté slowly in hot bacon fat. Turn once. Drain and then serve with salsa, curried mayonnaise, or a blue cheese dressing.
    Serves 4 at 18 cents each.

Majorcan Peas

4 slices bacon
6 green onions, chopped
3 cups fresh peas or 16 oz. frozen peas
1 bay leaf

Fry bacon and remove to drain. Add onions; cook for two minutes. Then add peas and bay leaf. Cook 20 minutes. Remove bay leaf. Crumble bacon and stir back into peas. Serve.
Serves 4 at 32 cents each.

French Peas

2 tbsp. butter
2 green onions, chopped
1 small head Boston lettuce, shredded
 pinch of sugar
16 oz. frozen peas
1/2 tsp. thyme

Sauté onions in butter for 5 minutes. Add lettuce and cook for 1 minute, until wilted. Add sugar, peas, and thyme. Cook four or five minutes.
Serves 4 at 32 cents each.

Note: Use fresh peas only during the season, which runs from April to July. Otherwise, frozen peas will be cheaper and may well taste better than fresh. Fresh peas are costly to store and transport.

Tarragon Green Beans

1 lb. fresh green beans
1 tbsp. butter
1/4 cup heavy cream
1/4 tsp. tarragon

Snap off ends of green beans; wash and drain. Cook in boiling water for 8 to 9 minutes. Save water for stock. Dry green beans over high heat for 30 seconds; add butter. Reduce heat and add cream. Simmer for 5 minutes, then increase heat if necessary to reduce the cream. Add tarragon.
　　Serves 4 for 26 cents each.

Szechuan Green Beans

1 lb. green beans
1/4 lb. ground meat–beef, pork, or turkey
1 tsp. ginger
1 tbsp. sugar
1 tbsp. soy sauce

Deep fry green beans until they wrinkle. If you have one, a wok makes an excellent deep fryer. Drain on paper towels. Save oil for future uses, leaving only a thin film in the wok. Add the meat and other ingredients, stir frying over high heat. When all the liquid has evaporated, pour the meat over the beans.
　　Serves 4 at 32 cents each.

Spinach Soufflé

3 tbsp. butter
3 tbsp. flour
1/3 cup heavy cream
2/3 cup vegetable stock
1 cup cooked spinach, minced or puréed
3 eggs, separated
nutmeg & white pepper
1/4 cup grated Parmesan cheese

Blend flour into melted butter over low heat. Slowly stir in cream and stock and cook, stirring, for 5 minutes. Stir in spinach and cheese, reduce heat, and add beaten egg yolks. Stir for 1 minute. Season with nutmeg and white pepper. Let mixture cool. Whip the egg whites until stiff, then fold them into the spinach. Pour into a greased baking dish and bake in a 350° oven for 40 minutes.
Serves 4 at 27 cents each.

If you pour the soufflé mixture into 4 individual ramekins, it is easier to make a grand presentation. You may need to reduce cooking time by as much as 10 minutes in that event. Other vegetable soufflés can be made by using the same recipe but replacing the 1 cup spinach, the Parmesan cheese, and the nutmeg with:

Carrot soufflé: 1 cup cooked shredded carrots, 1/4 cup dry breadcrumbs, and mace.
Asparagus soufflé: 1 cup cooked asparagus stems, shredded or puréed, and 1/4 cup grated Swiss cheese.
Corn soufflé: 3/4 cup creamed corn and 1/4 cup grated cheddar cheese.

Vegetable Stir Fry

3 green onions, chopped
1 cup chopped broccoli florets
2 carrots, sliced thin diagonally
1 small parsnip, sliced thin diagonally
1 small zucchini, sliced thin
2 tbsp. oil
Chinese 5 spice

Have all vegetables cut ahead of time. Sauté carrots and onions in the oil in a wok or skillet. Add broccoli, zucchini, and parsnip after a couple of minutes. Sprinkle on Chinese 5 spice. Lower heat and cover wok, allowing vegetables to steam 2 or 3 minutes. All vegetables should be cooked, but none of them limp.

Serves 4 at 20 cents each.

Variations: Use whatever vegetable odds and ends you have on hand. Just be sure to cut, slice, chop, or shred the vegetable so that it will cook quickly. Other possibilities: cauliflower, leeks, turnips, asparagus, celery, cabbage, okra, mushrooms, and green peppers.

Baked Onions

4 large onions
2 tbsp. butter
1/2 cup stock
1/2 cup dry white wine
2 tbsp. chopped parsley

Peel onions; set in baking dish. Heat butter, stock, and wine until butter dissolves. Add wine and parsley; pour over onions. Cover and bake at 350° for 90 minutes.
Serves 4 at 20 cents each.

Creamed Onions

16 small white onions
1/2 cup chicken or vegetable stock
1 cup tomato cream sauce (see page 149)
grated gruyére cheese

Boil unpeeled onions in water for 10 minutes. Drain off water. Let cool. Remove skins. Place onions in baking dish with tomato cream sauce; top with grated gruyére cheese and bake for 20 minutes.
Serves 4 at 32 cents each.

Variations: Use a cream sauce instead of the tomato cream sauce.
Top onions with bread crumbs mixed with butter and grated Parmesan cheese.
Cook onions for 30 minutes, then top with melted butter and sprinkle with cinnamon.

Great Zucchini!

4 green onions, chopped
2 green and 2 yellow zucchini, shredded
4 tbsp. butter
minced parsley
1 tsp. marjoram
1/4 cup grated Parmesan

Sauté onions in the butter. Add shredded zucchini, parsley, and marjoram. Cook quickly, as though you were making an omelet. Top with Parmesan.
Serves 4 for 35 cents each.

Steamed Artichokes

4 globe artichokes

Slice off stem of each artichoke flush with the base of its leaves. Cut off top inch of leaves, creating a flat top. Trim off thorn at the end of each leaf with scissors. Place artichokes, standing on their base, in one inch of boiling water. Squeeze the juice of one lemon over the artichokes. Simmer for 30 minutes. Drain and serve with melted butter and mayonnaise mixed with curry powder. (Eat the artichoke by peeling away the leaves, dipping them into the butter or mayonnaise, and biting off the meaty part at the bottom. When done with the leaves, scoop off the fuzz, revealing the heart at the base of the choke. Cut into bite sized pieces and eat with the butter or mayonnaise.)
Serves 4 for 75 cents each.

Caulimato Special

2 cups sliced cauliflower
2 ripe tomatoes, sliced
3 tbsp. butter
1/2 cup chopped onion
1/4 cup chopped parsley
1 tsp. oregano
1 cup half and half
1/4 cup flour
1 cup shredded Swiss cheese
1/2 cup bread or cracker crumbs

Sauté cauliflower 3 or 4 minutes in butter; add onion, parsley, and oregano. Cook another 4 or 5 minutes; add flour and half and half. Stir and cook to suitable consistency. Spoon cauliflower into shallow baking dish; top with tomatoes and then cheese; spoon another layer of cauliflower on top, followed by tomatoes and cheese; until all ingredients are exhausted. Sprinkle top with crumbs and bake at 400° for 25 minutes.
Serves 4 at 56 cents each.

You can vary the taste of this dish by using different kinds of bread or cracker crumbs for the topping: pumperknickel bread, crushed graham crackers, or a crumbled oatmeal muffin. Be creative!

Creole Lima Beans

16 oz. frozen lima beans
2 chopped green onions
1/4 cup chopped green pepper
1 cup tomato juice
1 1/2 tbsp. flour
Tabasco sauce

Cook lima beans according to directions on package. Meanwhile, sauté onions and pepper in a little bacon fat. Add flour, stirring to form a roux, and then tomato juice and Tabasco sauce (a splash or two). Add lima beans; simmer for 5 minutes.
Serves 4 at 23 cents each.

Pepper Rings

2 green peppers
1 batch stuffing (see page 74, cut recipe in half)

Remove core from green peppers; blanch in boiling water for 5 minutes. Let cool. Fill each pepper with prepared stuffing. Bake 15 minutes at 350°. Slice with sharp knife into 1/4-inch slices and serve stuffed rings.
Serves 4 at 18 cents each.

Variations: You can stuff a green, red, or yellow pepper with just about anything imaginable, from sloppy joe stuffing to curried rice. Or pour soufflé ingredients into peppers and bake them.

Carrot Pie

3/4 cup sugar
1/2 tsp. nutmeg
1 tsp. each cinnamon and ground ginger
1/8 tsp. ground cloves
1/2 tsp. grated lemon peel
2 eggs
2 cups carrots
1 cup evaporated milk
9-inch pie shell (see page 131)

Peel carrots and cut in chunks. Simmer 10 minutes in boiling water. Purée in blender or food processor. Beat eggs and blend into carrots. Add rest of ingredients and pour into the pie shell. Bake at 400° for 45 minutes.
 Serves 6 for 14 cents each.

Nutmeg Snaps

1 lb. green beans
3 tbsp. butter
1/4 tsp. nutmeg
1/8 tsp. pepper

Clean beans and snap off tips. Place in boiling water; simmer for 12 minutes. Drain (reserve water for vegetable stock) and add butter or margarine, nutmeg, and pepper. Toss until beans are dry.
 Serves 4 at 36 cents each.

Cabbage in Cabbage

1 1/2 lb. head of green cabbage
6 tbsp. butter
1 medium onion, minced
1 tbsp. chopped parsley
bread crumbs
2 eggs, lightly beaten
nutmeg

Discard any wilted outer leaves of cabbage. Peel off and reserve 5 perfect leaves. Remove core, then slice and chop the rest of the cabbage finely. Sauté chopped cabbage in butter, stirring often, for 30 minutes over low heat. Add onion and parsley, simmer another 10 minutes. While this is cooling, add to it the eggs and pinch of ntumeg. Drape a piece of cheesecloth in a large bowl; arrange the perfect leaves on top of the cheesecloth so they overlap. Spoon in chopped cabbage and draw up cheesecloth, fastening tightly. Drop cabbage into boiling water, simmer for 1 hour, turning once. Upwrap the cabbage and serve with more melted butter.

Serves 4 for 18 cents each.

Desserts

Although dessert is an "extra treat" that could easily be dispensed with, why should it be? There are plenty of desserts that can be fixed inexpensively. And there is nothing like a dessert to remind us that even if the budget is tight, we have a lot to be thankful for–and optimistic about.

As always, the key is to make your own. Why buy an apple pie in the store for $3.99 or more, when you can make a much better one yourself for $1.36 or less? That's for the whole pie! Cut it into 8 slices, and you are spending only 17 cents a serving.

This philosophy must go all the way down to the crust. It can cost $1.05 to buy a prepared double pie crust in the store. It costs only 32 cents to make one yourself. If your dessert calls for a graham cracker or vanilla wafer crust, why not use your own sugar cookies instead? It's an easy way to save money.

In selecting the recipes for this book, I have chosen only those that serve up a luscious dessert for less than 25 cents a serving.

Some of the best desserts are the simplest ones–a wedge or slice of fruit and a cookie or two. Recipes for cookies appear on pages 134. Here are some suggestions for serving fruit and other simple desserts:

A slice of fresh pineapple, with the center filled with blueberries, blackberries, or sliced strawberries and topped with a sprinking of sugar. Or fill the center with a dollop of whipped cream or yogurt. Cost: 21 cents.

One half of a grapefruit, cored and filled with a tablespoon of brown sugar and a splash of sherry, and browned under the broiler for 30 seconds. Be sure to loosen the fruit from the grapefruit's membranes, so it is easier to eat. No one likes to fight his or her dessert!
Cost: 19 cents a serving.

Peel and slice a banana lengthwise. Sauté on low heat, cut side down, in 1 tablespoon butter. Chop up two dried apricot halves and add to butter. After turning the banana, dust the top side with brown sugar, sprinkle with lemon juice, and flambé with a splash of rum. Serve with the apricot bits on top of the banana.
Cost: 21 cents a serving.

One of the classic desserts is made by coring and slicing an apple and serving it with slices of cheddar or colby cheese. One good-sized apple served in this way is enough for two people. Cost: 18 cents.

Or, just serve an array of cheeses and nuts, especially if the main course of the meal has been heavy.

Shortcake Supreme

Prepare shortcake dough as described on page 36, then add 1/2 cup chopped pecans. Cut the dough into 3-inch wide rounds. Bake as directed. Split in half and butter. Cover bottom half with a mixture of sliced strawberries and bananas that has been sugared and sitting at least 30 minutes. Add top half of biscuit, then more fruit. If desired, top with whipped cream.

Makes 8 servings at 25 cents each.

Variations: Use whatever berries and fruits happen to be the best buys at the time. Peaches also make an excellent shortcake.

Chocolate Mousse

1 small orange and 1 banana
1/2 cup sugar
6 oz. semi-sweet chocolate (can use chips)
2 eggs, plus 2 egg yolks
1 cup heavy cream
1/2 tsp. vanilla extract

Grate 1 teaspoon of orange rind; combine it with sugar, two whole eggs, beaten, and two egg yolks, beaten. Beat until frothy. Add melted chocolate and 1 tablespoon orange juice. Blend in. Add banana, thinly sliced. Whip cream with vanilla extract until stiff; fold in. Pour into individual serving glasses; chill. When ready to serve, place an orange segment on top of each mousse.

Serves 8 at 22 cents each.

If the budget allows, substitute fresh red raspberries for the sliced bananas.

127

Miracle Cake

2 cups flour
1 cup sugar
4 tbsp. cocoa
1 1/2 tsp. baking powder
1 1/2 tsp. soda
1 cup Miracle Whip™ salad dressing

Sift or blend thoroughly the dry ingredients. Make a well in the center of them. Add Miracle Whip and 1 cup water. Mix thoroughly and pour into 2 nine-inch buttered layer cake pans. Bake at 350° for 35 minutes. Ice while warm with chocolate frosting.

Serves 8 at 20 cents each. A comparable cake, made from a mix, would cost at least 30 cents a serving.

Chocolate Frosting: Melt 3 oz. chocolate with 3 tablespoons butter. Remove from heat and add one beaten egg. Gradually add 1 teaspoon vanilla and up to 2 cups confectioner's sugar, until you achieve the right consistency. Makes enough frosting for Miracle Cake.

Seven from Heaven

Melt 1 stick of butter in a 9 x 12 cake pan. Layer by layer, add 1 cup graham cracker crumbs, 1 cup shredded coconut, 6 ounces of chocolate chips, 6 ounces of butterscotch bits, 1 small can condensed milk, and 3/4 cup chopped walnuts or pecans. Bake at 350° for 30 minutes. For best results, make a day before serving.

Makes 18 bars at 17 cents apiece.

Chocolate Waffles

1 cup cake flour
1 tsp. baking powder
1/2 tsp. salt
1/4 tsp. cinnamon
2 beaten eggs plus 2 egg whites, stiffly beaten
1 cup heavy cream
2 ounces bittersweet chocolate, melted
6 tbsp. sugar

Sift together the flour, baking powder, cinnamon, and salt. Add 2 beaten eggs and 1 cup heavy cream. Stir until smooth; add chocolate and sugar. Fold in egg whites. Bake in waffle iron. Serve with a small scoop of vanilla ice cream in the center of each waffle; top with hot fudge sauce.

Serves 8 at 25 cents each.

Hot Fudge Sauce: Add 1 tablespoon butter to 2 ounces unsweetened chocolate. Blend in 1/3 cup boiling water, stir, and add 1 cup sugar and 2 tablespoons corn syrup. Boil gently for 5 to 8 minutes.

Variations: Substitute banana slices for the ice cream; top with hot fudge sauce.

Or, for a simpler dessert, just sprinkle powdered sugar over each waffle while still hot.

Cost: 8 cents per waffle square.

Dutch Family Cake

1/2 cup butter or shortening
2 oz. chocolate
1 cup sugar
2 eggs
1 cup apple sauce
1 tsp. vanilla
1/2 cup pecans, chopped
1 cup flour
1/2 tsp. baking powder
1/4 tsp. each baking soda and salt

Melt butter and chocolate. Cool. Stir in sugar, eggs, apple sauce, vanilla, and pecans. Sift together dry ingredients, stir into chocolate. Pour into 8-inch square greased pan. Bake at 350° for 35 to 40 minutes. Requires no icing. Sprinkle top with powdered sugar.
Serves 9 people at 12 cents each.

Shortbread

1 lb. softened butter
8 cups flour
1 1/2 cups sugar
1 egg

Cut butter and flour together until mixture resembles coarse sand. Add sugar and beaten egg; mix well. Knead and roll into large cakes 1/2-inch thick. Prick each piece several times with a fork. Bake at 300° for 20 to 30 minutes. Makes 64 servings at 3 cents each.

Pumpkin Pie

1 can (29 oz.) pumpkin
3 cups heavy cream
1 cup brown sugar
1/2 cup white sugar
1 tsp. salt
2 tsp. cinnamon
1 tsp. ginger
1/4 tsp. cloves
8 slighty beaten eggs
2 tsp. vanilla
2 unbaked pie crusts

Combine all ingredients except the crust, blending until smooth. Pour into crust and bake at 425° for 15 minutes; reduce to 350° and bake another 25 to 30 minutes. Pie is done when knife inserted into center of filling comes out clean. Makes 2 pies.
   Serves 16 at 22 cents each.

Crust: Sift 2 cups flour with 1 teaspoon salt. Blend 1/3 cup shortening and 1/3 cup butter together; let stand until they are room temperature. Then cut the butter-shortening into the flour with a pastry blender, until the dough resembles gravel. Sprinkle the dough with 5 tablespoons water. Shape it into a ball. Divide dough in two. Roll both out into thin circles. Lay each circle of dough in a pie pan. Press down to make dough fit snugly into pan. Cut off excess dough and crimp edges. Makes two crusts.

Apple Pie

6 cups peeled, sliced cooking apples
1 tbsp. lemon juice
1/2 cup sugar
1/2 cup brown sugar
2 tbsp. flour
1/2 tsp. cinnamon
1/4 tsp. nutmeg
2 tbsp. butter
pastry for 2 pie crusts (see page 131)

Roll pastry for bottom crust out to 1/8-inch thickness, 1/2-inch larger than the pie pan. Lay gently in pan, pressing down to make a smooth fit. Spread apples on top of pie shell. Combine rest of ingredients (except butter), stirring well. Spoon over apples, distributing liquid equally. Dot top of apples with butter. Roll out pastry for top crust; set in place. Trim off excess pastry. Fold edges under and flute. Cut slits in top of pie to let steam escape. Brush top with milk, then sprinkle with sugar. You may also want to cover the pastry edges with strips of aluminum foil, to prevent burning. Bake at 450° for 15 minutes; reduce heat to 350° and bake another 35 minutes.

Serves 8 at 17 cents each.

Shoo Fly Pie

2 cups flour
1/2 cup sugar
1/3 cup shortening or butter
1 cup molasses or corn syrup (or 1/2 of each)
1 tsp. baking soda
pastry for 1 pie crust

Sift flour and sugar together, then cut in shortening to make fine crumbs. Beat molasses and baking soda with 1 cup warm water. Fill pie shell with alternating layers of molasses and crumbs, ending with the crumbs on top. Bake at 425° for 10 minutes, then finish baking at 350°–until filling is firm. Serves 8 for 10 cents each.

Coconut Mousse Pie

1 cup heavy cream
3 tbsp. sugar
1/2 tsp. vanilla
1 stiff egg white
1/2 cup shredded coconut, toasted
cookie pie crust for 8-inch pan

Whip cream; add sugar and vanilla. Fold in egg white and coconut. Chill until thick. Pour into graham cracker crust; top with fresh strawberries, bananas, or kiwi.
Serves 8 at 16 cents each, plus fruit.

cookie pie crust: Combine 1 2/3 cups crushed sugar cookiess with 1/4 cup sugar and 6 tablespoons margarine. Press into pie plate. Bake at 350° for 7 minutes.

133

Sugar: Sift together 2 1/2 cups flour, 1/2 teaspoon cream of tartar, 1/2 teaspoon soda, and 1/4 teaspoon salt. In a separate bowl, combine 1/2 cup shortening with 1 cup sugar, 1 beaten egg, 1/3 cup milk, and 1 teaspoon vanilla extract. Blend. Gradually add the flour mixture, until thoroughly mixed. Place dough on a lightly floured board; divide in half. Roll out each ball to 1/8 inch thickness, then cut into desired shapes. Bake at 400° for 5 to 7 minutes on an ungreased baking sheet. Makes 60 cookies at less than one cent each.

Oatmeal: Cream 1/2 cup butter with 1/2 cup each brown and white sugar. Add, beating until smooth, 1 egg, 1 teaspoon vanilla, and 1 tablespoon milk. Sift together 1 cup flour and 1/2 teaspoon each of soda, baking powder, and salt. Add to batter, beating until smooth. Add 1 cup uncooked quick oats. Drop cookies 2 inches apart on well-greased cookie sheet and bake at 350° until light brown, about 10 to 12 minutes. Makes 36 cookies at 2 cents each.

Oatmeal Raisin: add 3/4 cup raisins with the oatmeal.
Oatmeal Apricot: add 3/4 cup minced dried apricot.
Oatmeal Chocolate: add 3/4 cup chocolate chips.

Surprises: Beat 2 egg whites, 1/8 teaspoon salt, 1/8 teaspoon cream of tartar, and 1 teaspoon vanilla until soft peaks rise. Add 3/4 cup sugar slowly, beating until peaks stiffen. Fold in 6 ounces of semisweet chocolate chips and 1/4 cup finely chopped walnuts. Cover cookie sheet with aluminum foil. Drop by rounded teaspoons two inches apart. Bake at 300° for 25 minutes. Makes 2 dozen at 5 cents each.

Baked Atlanta

2 eggs
3/4 cup sugar
1/2 teaspoon cinnamon
1/2 cup flour
1/2 cup chopped pecans
1/2 cup raisins
1/4 cup rum
2 egg yolks, beaten
2 teaspoons vanilla extract
1/3 cup heavy cream, boiling

Beat eggs and 1 1/2 tablespoons sugar together. Add flour and 1 cup of water, mixing until smooth. Add cinnamon. Dropping batter 1/4 cup at a time on a hot griddle or skillet, make 4 crepes.

Mix pecans and raisins together. Sprinkle on 1 1/2 tablespoons sugar plus rum. Spread mixture on the four crepes; roll up and place in a deep baking dish.

Stir together egg yolks and remaining sugar (9 tablespoons) over low heat until creamy. Add vanilla extract. Stir in cream, beating until the sauce thickens to a custard consistency. Pour over crepes. Bake at 475° for 5 minutes, taking care the sauce does not curdle.

Serves 4 at 20 cents each.

Variations: Instead of raisins, use 1/2 cup of minced dried apricot or 1/2 cup mashed banana. Add grated orange peel to the batter. Use Grand Marnier instead of rum.

Or use filo pastry instead of the crepes.

Ice Box Pudding

1 cup vanilla wafer crumbs
1/2 cup chopped nuts
1/2 cup butter
1 cup powdered sugar
3 eggs, separated
1 1/2 ounces chocolate
1/2 tsp. vanilla

Mix crumbs and nuts, use half to line the bottom of a 6 x 9 pan (glass is best). Cream butter and sugar, add egg yolks, mixing thoroughly. Add melted chocolate and vanilla, blending in. Fold in stiffly beaten egg whites. Pour over crumbs, spreading until even. Add remaining crumbs on top. Refrigerate at least 8 hours.
Makes 10 servings at 14 cents each.

Lemon Soufflé

5 eggs, separated
3/4 cup sugar
1 tsp. grated lemon rind
1/4 cup lemon juice
1/2 cup finely chopped nuts

Beat egg yolks until light. Add sugar slowly, beating constantly until eggs are creamy. Add lemon rind, lemon juice, and nuts. Fold in stiffly beaten egg whites. Pour into one 8-inch soufflé dish or 4 individual dishes. Set in a pan of hot, but not boiling water, in a 350° oven for 35 minutes. Serve with cream.
Serves 4 at 18 cents each.

Breads

Bread is the mainstay of human life in virtually every cuisine on the planet. For this reason, if you are serious about saving money on your food budget, one of the best-and most delicious ways-to do this is to bake your own bread. This advice may seem odd, since it is possible to buy commercial loaves of bread for as little as 3 1/2 cents a slice. But it is possible to make a much better loaf of bread yourself for as little as 1 1/2 cents a slice.

How important are these two cents? If a family of four consumes 24 slices of bread per day, it would save a minimum of 50 cents a day or $185 a year by baking its own. If you pay more than the absolute minimum for bread, your savings will be more in the range of $225 to $300. If you buy whole wheat and oat bran breads, your savings will be on the order of $370 a year.

Here are some other examples of savings:

It costs 20 cents to buy one pita round in the store. You can make it yourself for 4 cents a round.

You can buy brown and serve rolls for 12 cents each. You can bake better dinner rolls for 2 cents each.

All in all, a family of 4 should be able to save over $500 a year just by baking its own bread.

White Bread

2 tsp. yeast (1 pkg.)
2 cups lukewarm milk
2 tbsp. melted butter or shortening
2 tsp. salt
2 tbsp. sugar
6 to 7 cups flour

Dissolve yeast and sugar in 1/4 cup warm water. Add milk, butter, salt, and sugar, stirring well. Stir in 3 cups of flour, one cup at a time, stirring with each addition. Add 4th cup of flour, beating until smooth and elastic. Rest if your hand tires. Add 5th cup of flour; mix until dough is stiff. Sprinkle half of the 6th cup on a pastry board. Turn dough out onto board. With floured hands, begin kneading dough, adding more flour whenever the process gets a little sticky. In order to knead, shape dough into a ball. Press down with your palms to flatten the ball; fold one side up over the other, like an omelet. Turn dough 90 degrees, fold again. Begin kneading process again. Kneading cannot be timed. It will be done when the dough becomes smooth and easy to handle. Put dough in greased bowl, greasing the top of the ball slighty. Let rise for 1 1/2 hours in a warm place, until doubled in bulk. Punch down dough, squeezing out air bubbles. Shape into a smooth ball; divide into two loaves. Place loaves in greased bread pans. Let rise 45 minutes, then bake at 375° for 45 minutes. Makes 2 loaves at 2 cents a slice.

Rye Bread: Substitute rye flour for 2 cups of the white flour. Add 2 tablespoons grated orange peel and 1 tablespoon caraway seed.

Serene Bread

4 tsp. dry yeast (2 pkgs.) plus 2 tbsp. sugar
1 beaten egg
1/4 cup melted butter
1 1/2 tsp. salt
1/2 cup sugar (or part sugar, part honey)
4 cups whole wheat flour & 4 cups white flour

Dissolve yeast and sugar in 1/2 cup lukewarm water. Beat together the egg, butter, 2 1/2 cups lukewarm water, salt, and sugar. Combine with yeast mixture. Add flour and stir until a stiff dough results. Turn onto a floured board. Knead for 10 minutes. Place in an oiled bowl, cover with a towel, and let rise until doubled in bulk. Punch down and divide dough into three balls. Shape loaves to fit in 5 x 9 loaf pans. Let rise again until doubled in bulk. Place in cold oven. Bake at 400° for 15 minutes, then reduce heat to 350°, baking 25 minutes longer. Makes 3 loaves at 2 cents a slice.

Flour Tortillas

3 1/2 cups flour
1 tsp. salt and 1 tsp. baking powder
1/3 cup shortening
1 cup lukewarm milk

Combine flour, salt, and baking powder; cut in shortening. Add milk. Knead dough 3 minutes. Roll out to 8-inch circles. Cook tortillas 2 minutes on each side in an ungreased skillet. Makes 10 tortillas at 4 cents each.

Sourdough French Bread

Sourdough is the least expensive form of bread, as it replaces yeast with, well, sour dough. To bake sourdough bread, it is therefore necessary to maintain an active, fresh supply of sourdough starter.

To make starter, place 1 cup milk in a jar or crock (not a can or pot) and let it stand at room temperature for 24 hours. Stir in 1 cup flour. Leave uncovered in a warm place for 2 to 5 days, until it becomes bubbly.

Every time you use part of your starter, replenish it with a mixture of equal amounts of milk and flour. Leave at room temperature overnight, then refrigerate. Always try to use starter at least once a week, or at least replenish it, so that it stays fresh. If you follow these simple rules, your starter will last years and years, ready to serve you daily, if you bake that often.

1 cup starter
6 cups flour
2 tsp. each sugar and salt
1/2 tsp. soda

Combine starter, 4 cups flour, salt, sugar, and 1 1/2 cups warm water in a bowl. Cover and leave at room temperature 18 hours. Mix soda with 1 cup flour; stir into sour mass. Turn dough onto pastry board and knead, adding remaining 1 cup flour as needed. Knead until dough cannot absorb any more flour. Shape into 2 French loaves; place on a lightly greased baking sheet, cover with a towel, and let rise (3 to 4 hours). Brush with water; make diagonal slices on top with a sharp knife. Bake at 400° until dark brown–50 minutes.

Makes 2 loaves at 15 cents each.

Finnish Bread

2 tbsp. butter
1 tbsp. sugar
2 tsp. salt
2 tsp. yeast
3 cups rye flour (or whole wheat)
2 1/2 cups white flour

Stir butter, sugar, and salt into 1 1/2 cups hot water. Let it cool to lukewarm. Dissolve yeast in 1/2 cup lukewarm water. Let sit 5 minutes, then blend it into first mixture. Stir in rye flour; beat with a wooden spoon for 1 minute. Add 2 cups white flour; blend. Turn out onto a floured pastry board. Knead for 10 minutes, adding more flour if necessary. Place dough in a greased bowl. Brush top with melted butter, cover with a towel, and let it rise until doubled in bulk, about 1 hour. Punch down and knead lightly. Divide dough in half and shape each half into a round loaf. Place on greased baking sheet. Press down on dough so it is only about 1 inch thick. Cover and let rise about 45 minutes. Bake at 400° for 25 to 30 minutes. Serve in wedges, pie-like.
Makes 16 wedges at 4 cents each.

To make this as a sourdough bread, replace the yeast with 1 teaspoon soda and use 1 cup starter in place of 3/4 to 1 cup flour. Begin by combining 4 cups of flour, the starter and 1 1/2 cups of water and letting it sit, covered, for 18 to 24 hours at room temperature. Then combine rest of the ingredients, except flour, and stir in. The rest of the flour is kneaded into the dough on the pastry board. Also remember that the second proofing will take longer than with yeast bread.

Cranberry Nut Bread

2 cups flour
1/2 tsp. each salt, soda, and baking powder
2 tbsp. melted butter
1 cup sugar
1 egg, beaten
1 cup chopped cranberries
1/2 cup orange juice
1/2 cup chopped nuts
grated rind of an orange

Sift flour, salt, sugar, baking powder, and soda together. Add egg, juice, butter, and 2 tablespoons hot water. Add cranberries. Blend quickly, then fold in nuts and orange rind. Place dough in a greased loaf pan and bake at 325° for 75 minutes. Makes 1 loaf for 90 cents.

Variations: Use apricots or prunes in place of the cranberries.

Banana Bread: Follow recipe as above, but substitute 3 mashed bananas for the cranberries and 1/2 cup sour milk for the juice. Omit orange rind. Bake at 350° for 1 hour.

English Muffins

1/2 cup milk
2 tsp. sugar
1 tsp. salt
2 tsp. yeast
4 cups flour
3 tbsp. softened butter

Combine milk, sugar, and salt with one cup hot water in one bowl, while dissolving yeast in 2 tablespoons water in another. Combine the two mixtures. Beat in 2 cups flour. Cover bowl with towel and let rise 90 minutes. Beat in butter, then knead in remaining flour. Roll out dough to 3/4 inch thickness; cut 2 1/2-inch circles from dough and place on a piece of waxed paper sprinkled with cornmeal. Sprinkle tops with more cornmeal, let rise again. Cook on a griddle, turning once.
Makes 20 muffins at 2 cents each.

Pita Bread

6 cups flour
1 tbsp. sugar
2 tsp. each yeast and salt

Mix 2 cups flour with other ingredients. Gradually add 2 cups warm water. Stir in more flour to make a soft dough. Knead for 10 minutes. Set in greased bowl; cover; and let rise for an hour. Punch down; reshape. Cover and let sit 30 minutes. Divide into 6 parts. Roll each into an 8-inch diameter round. Place each on a greased cookie sheet. Bake at 450° for 5 minutes.

2 tsp. yeast
2 eggs, plus enough milk to make 2 cups liquid
1/2 cup melted butter
1 1/2 tsp. salt
1/2 cup sugar
6 cups flour

Combine ingredients as you would for bread. Blend in 5 cups of flour; knead in the last cup. Let rise; punch down; and shape into rolls. Place in muffin tins or on baking sheets; cover with towel and let rise again. Bake at 425° for 10 minutes.
Makes 60 rolls at 1 cent each.

Common shapes:
Crescent Rolls–roll dough into 8-inch circles, 1/4-inch thick. Brush with butter. Cut in wedges. Roll each wedge toward its tip. Curve roll to make a crescent shape. Place on greased pan, point down.

Fan Rolls: Roll dough to 8 x 15-inch rectangle, 1/4 inch thick. Spread with butter; cut into 5 lengthwise strips. Stack and cut into squares. Put in greased muffin cups with a cut side up, so it can fan outward.

Snail Rolls: Roll dough by hand into a rope about 1/2 inch in diameter and 10 inches long. Starting with one end, wrap rope around an imaginary central point, spiraling outward until it is a good-sized roll.

Blueberry Squares

2 cups flour
2 tsp. baking powder
1/4 tsp. salt
1/4 cup shortening
3/4 cup sugar
1 egg, well beaten
1/2 cup milk
1 tsp. vanilla extract
1 1/4 cup fresh blueberries

Sift or stir together 1 3/4 cups flour, baking powder, and salt. Mix sugar into shortening, stirring. Add egg; beat well. Combine milk and vanilla; add to sugar-egg mixture along with flour mixture, alternating between the two and beating after each addition. Toss blueberries lightly with remaining flour; fold into batter. Pour into a greased and floured 8 x 8 pan. Bake at 350° for 60 minutes. Makes 9 squares at 12 cents each.

Oatmeal Muffins

Soak 1 cup oatmeal in 1 cup sour milk for an hour. Add 1 beaten egg and stir. Add 1/2 cup brown sugar and 1/2 cup melted and cooled shortening. Add 1 cup flour sifted with 1/2 teaspoon salt, 1 teaspoon baking powder, and 1/2 teaspoon soda. Mix briefly. Spoon into greased muffin tins and bake at 400° for 10 to 12 minutes.
Makes 12 muffins at 5 cents each.

Pasta

3 cups flour
4 eggs
2 tsp. salt
4 tsp. oil

Pour the flour on a pastry board so that it makes a well in the center. Drop into it the eggs mixed with the salt, oil, and 1 tablespoon water. Fold the flour into the eggs, shaping it gradually into a ball of dough that does not stick to your hands. Knead the dough for 10 minutes. Let it stand, covered by a towel, for 1 hour. Roll the dough out, pulling it and stretching it. Sprinkle on a little more flour every time the dough is stretched. Repeat 10 to 12 times, until the dough has become very thin and translucent. Let it dry for 30 minutes like a towel on a line. Before it becomes brittle, roll it up like a scroll, and cut it on the diagonal. The width of the strips determines what kind of pasta it is. Very thin is angel hair. Thin is spaghetti. Moderate is linguini. Wide is fettucine. For ravioli, cut into 3-inch squares. For cannelloni, cut into 4-inch squares. For lasagna, cut into 3 x 6-inch rectangles. To cook, place pasta in rapidly boiling water and let boil 3 to 5 minutes, or until al dente.
   Makes 10 servings of dry pasta, at 4 cents each.

Variations: Use whole wheat flour instead of white.
   For green pasta, add 1/4 cup finely minced cooked spinach when dough is almost ready to be set aside.
   For red pasta, add 1/4 cup tomato paste at the same time.

Homemade Everything

The more you experiment in the kitchen, the more you will find that almost anything that can be bought at the store can be made in the home. It will cost less and deliver more taste.

In fact, many of the items I have included in this final set of recipes are prohibitively expensive if bought as a commercial product. But when it is produced in your own kitchen, the price becomes reasonable.

Dressings & Sauces

See page 51 for the basic recipe for mayonnaise, page 52 for a recipe for a curry dressing, page 54 for a Louis dressing, and page 55 for a tarragon mayonnaise.

These dressings can be refrigerated for 1 to 2 weeks.

1000 Island. Combine 1 cup mayonnaise with 1/4 cup chili sauce, 1/2 tbsp. minced onion, 1 tbsp. minced green pepper, 1 tbsp. minced pimento, 1/8 cup sweet pickle relish, and 1 finely chopped hard boiled egg. Blend well. If too thick, thin with a little half and half. Cost: 7 cents an ounce.

Blue Cheese. Blend 1 cup sour cream, 4 ounces of blue cheese, 1/4 teaspoon of Worcestershire sauce, 1/4 teaspoon of garlic salt, and 1/2 tablespoon lemon juice. Cost: 13 cents an ounce.

French. Mix 1/2 cup salad oil with 1/4 cup red wine vinegar, 1 teaspoon minced garlic, and a dash of pepper. Cost: 3 cents an ounce.

Vinaigrette. Mix 1 tablespoon minced green onion with 1/2 cup salad oil, 3 tablespoons wine vinegar, and 1 tablespoon Dijon mustard. Cost: 3 cents an ounce.

Avocado. Slice and mash 1 ripe avocado. Beat with 1/4 cup lime juice, 1/4 teaspoon sugar, and 1 teaspoon minced garlic, until creamy. Cost: 6 cents an ounce.

Banana. Mash one overripe banana. Blend with 1/2 cup pineapple juice, 1/2 cup salad oil, and 1 table-spoon lemon juice, until puréed. Cost: 3 cents an ounce.

Slaw Dressing. Blend 1 cup mayonnaise with 4 chopped green onions, 1 tablespoon catsup, 2 teaspoons vinegar, 1/8 teaspoon Worcestershire, 1/8 teaspoon pepper, and 1/4 teaspoon sugar. Pour over slaw just before serving. Cost: 5 cents an ounce.

White Sauce. Add 1 1/2 tablespoons flour to 1 1/2 tablespoons melted butter, stirring. Add 1 cup milk a little at a time, stirring to prevent lumping. Continue stirring until sauce boils. Cook 5 to 10 minutes more at very low heat. Yield: 1 cup for 2 cents an ounce.

Cheese Sauce: Add 1 cup shredded cheese and 1/4 teaspoon dry mustard to basic white sauce.

Dill Sauce: Add 1 teaspoon each lemon juice and dried dill weed to basic white sauce. Stir.

Tomato Cream Sauce. Sauté 3 chopped green onions in 2 tablespoons olive oil. Add 1 can (28 oz.) of crushed tomatoes and 2 tablespoons tomato paste. Add 1 teaspoon garlic flakes, 1 teaspoon oregano, and 2 teaspoons basil. Bring to a boil, then simmer on low heat for 15 minutes. Add 1/2 cup cream. Simmer another 10 minutes. Makes 3 1/2 cups sauce for 90 cents. Use with pasta, on pizza, or on meat loaf. For a stronger sauce, omit or reduce cream.

Hollandaise Sauce: Melt 12 tablespoons butter over low heat. Separate 3 eggs, saving the whites for another use and putting the yolks into the container of a blender. Add 1 tablespoon lemon juice and a dash of cayenne pepper. Blend on low speed. Uncover and pour butter in a steady stream. When sauce is smooth, stop blending. Makes 1 cup for 7 cents an ounce.

Maltaise Sauce: Stir 1 tablespoon orange juice and 2 teaspoons grated orange rind into 1 cup hollandaise.

Bearnaise: Pour freshly made hollandaise back into blender. Simmer 2 tablespoons tarragon vinegar, 2 tablespoons dry white wine, 1 tablespoon fresh tarragon, and 1 tablespoon chopped green onion until almost dry. Spoon residue into hollandaise and blend on high speed for 6 seconds.

Tartar Sauce: Blend 2 tablespoons sweet pickle relish with 1 teaspoon dried parsley flakes, 1 table-spoon grated onion, 1 tablespoon lemon juice, a dash of Tabasco, and 2/3 cup mayonnaise (see page 51). Cover and chill before using.

Barbeque Sauce: Sauté 1 chopped onion and 2 cloves of garlic in 2 tablespoons butter. Add 1 cup catsup, 1 cup water, 3/4 cup chili sauce, 1/4 cup brown sugar, 2 tablespoons Dijon mustard, 2 tablespoons Worcestershire sauce, and a dash of Tabasco. Bring to a boil; simmer 10 to 15 minutes. Store in refrigerator. Makes 3 cups for 3 cents an ounce.

Cocktail Sauce: Combine 1 cup tomato-based chili sauce with 2 tablespoon horseradish, 2 tablespoons fresh lemon juice, 2 teaspoons Worcestershire, and 1/4 teaspoon cayenne pepper. Refrigerate.

Hot Sauce: Chop 2 ripe tomatoes and combine with 1/2 cup chopped sweet onion, 1/2 cup chopped peeled cucumber, 1/2 cup chopped green pepper, 1 tablespoon minced jalapeño, and 1 tablespoon apple cider vinegar, Let sit at least 20 minutes before serving.

Butters

Honey Butter: Blend 1 stick butter with with 1/4 cup honey and 1 teaspoon cinnamon. Great on toast!

Chive Butter: Blend 1 stick softened butter with 2 tablespoons fresh minced chives. Great on steak.
Or replace the chives with 2 teaspoons of dried basil,oregano, tarragon, or chervil, as desired. Chill.

Almond Butter: Soften 1 stick of butter. Blanch 1/2 cup slivered almonds. Pound to a paste, adding 1 teaspoon water. Blend with butter. Chill.

Condiments

Cranberry Sauce. Dissolve 2 cups sugar in 2 cups water; bring to a boil. Boil 5 minutes. Add 4 cups of cranberries. Simmer without stirring for 5 minutes. Skim surface, then add 2 teaspoons grated orange rind. Chill until ready to serve.

Guacamole. Peel, pit, and cut up 2 avocados. Place chunks in blender with 4 chopped green onions, 1 small tomato, chopped, 1 teaspoon Worcestershire sauce, and 1 tablespoon lime juice. Blend for a few seconds, until smooth and creamy. Serves 4 at 30 cents each.

Vanilla Extract. Slice a vanilla bean lengthwise. Place in 1/4 cup of rum or vodka. Cover tightly. Shake occasionally for six weeks. Discard bean, leaving you with vanilla extract. Cost: 4 cents per serving.

Coffee. If you can buy it in bulk at a wholesale club, it can cost as little as 1 cent a cup. Instant coffee will be much more expensive.

Tea. If you buy the family tea bags, the price can be as low as 1 cent a cup.

Iced Tea. Brew regular tea. While still hot, pour over a tall glass filled with ice cubes–and a slice of lemon rind or a mint leaf, if desired. Cost: 1 cent a serving.

Cocoa. Because cocoa mixes are so inexpensive, it is not reasonable to make your own from scratch.
Cost: 4 cents.

Orange Juice. The farther you live from Florida, the more you will have to rely on concentrate. In Atlanta, it is often possible to buy fresh orange juice for 11 cents a glass. From concentrate: 9 cents a glass.

Smoothie. In a blender, combine 1/2 cup orange juice with a scoop of vanilla ice cream, a half a small banana, sliced, and 3 ice cubes. Blend. Cost: 15 cents.

Sangría. Peel and slice 1 banana, 1 peach, and 1 orange. Slice a half dozen strawberries. Add fruit to 1 bottle of dry red wine and 1/2 cup sugar. Marinate for at least 30 minutes. To serve, add 2/3 quart lemon soda and 12 ice cubes. Serve in tall glasses. Cost: 30 cents a glass.

The $1.98 Challenge

I always knew, somewhere in the recesses of my awareness, that I could cook for less. I always thought, however, that the savings would be minor–a dime here, a few pennies there. Nothing much.

Then I began to put this book together. And I discovered how much money I waste each year by not practicing good economy in the kitchen.

I am not referring to eating chicken instead of veal. Those are choices which will be determined by your overall budget. I am referring to the money that can be saved by:

· Making your own hash browns or shoestrings instead of buying them frozen at the grocery. The average Orelda™ product sells for $1.15 a pound in the freezer section. In the produce department, raw potatoes sell for 16 cents a pound. You can save 99 cents (or more) on every pound of potatoes you consume.

· Making your own dinner rolls instead of buying them premade at the store. A crescent dinner roll may cost 15 cents at the store. You can make them for 1 penny apiece.

· Making your own French toast or pancakes in the morning, instead of buying the kind you heat up in the toaster.

· Making your own soup stocks, instead of buying the canned stuff in the stores.

There are hundreds and even thousands of dollars that every family can save each year–not by changing their diet or eating inferior foods, but just by deciding not to buy highly processed food items.

By deciding to make pizza and tacos at home, instead of bringing them home from the grocery.

By deciding to bake their own bread, instead of buying it at the store.

By saving leftovers and using them as the basis for another meal–for instance, an omelet for lunch.

By fixing oatmeal from scratch (at 8 cents a serving), instead of buying it in convenience packs (as much as $1.69 a serving).

Of course, there are other ways to save money, too. If you have the room to cultivate a vegetable garden, this can help you realize enormous savings on things you can grow on your own–especially otherwise expensive items such as asparagus.

But not all of us have the space or the time for gardens. Do not be discouraged. You can also save far more money than you knew possible, just by buying wisely and spending more time in the kitchen.

My original challenge to myself in writing this book was to spend no more than $1.98 on each dinner and a similar $1.98 on breakfast and lunch combined. This comes to a total of $3.96 a day. How did I do? In averaging the meals presented in this book, I found that the average cost for my recipes is:

Breakfast: 40 cents a person.

Lunch: 85 cents a person.

Dinner:

Entree–75 cents a person.

Vegetables–25 cents a person.

Potato–16 cents a person.

Bread–3 cents a person.

Dessert–17 cents a person

Or an average total of $2.61 per day. In fact, you would have to gorge yourself on the recipes in this book in order to equal my target goal of $3.96.

This brings up an interesting question. If the average cost of preparing three full, well-balanced meals a day, as described in this book, is only $2.61 a day, then why is the amount of food stamps given to single people as high as $3.69? Has the government accounting office crunched the same numbers I have? Perhaps we need a new generation of bean counters–ones who actually count beans! Or at least east them.

This leads to yet another question. If food stamp allotments provide 30 percent more buying power than what is required to eat extremely well, day in and day out, then why does anyone go hungry in this country? There can only be two answers: either they do not know how to apply for food stamps or they do not know how to shop and cook wisely on the allotment given them.

It is important to be very clear on this point. The recipes in this book are not built on cheap, unhealthy ingredients. I have not hesitated to use shrimp, even lobster in these dishes. The dishes I have described include some of the great achievements of the culinary art. And they fulfill the basic principle of good nutrition– a balanced diet with elements of all four food groups. Anyone in any income bracket should be more than satisfied with the quality and quantity of food suggested here. They are practical, sensible, and inexenaic

If these menus represent an average expense of 30 percent less than the daily allotment of food stamps in America, then something is wrong. Either there is a lot less hunger in America than we have been led to believe, or the programs aimed at ending hunger are woefully misdirected. Perhaps both.

But this is not the end of the story. I advertised in chapter one that I would show that it is possible to eat well on not $3.96 a day, not $3.69 a day, and not $2.61 a day–but on just $1.98 a day. Can it be done? Of course it can. Here's how:

Day One:
Breakfast–49 cents
Two eggs, 3 slices bacon, toast, grits, juice, coffee
Lunch–60 cents
Hamburger crunch, potato salad, iced tea,
cookiescookies
Dinner–82 cents
Turkey tetrazzini, rice pilaf, vegetable stir-fry, rolls,
hot tea, Dutch family cake
Total: $1.91

Day Two:
Breakfast–64 cents
Sausage biscuits, scrambled eggs, grapefruit, coffee
Lunch–68 cents
Curried lima bean soup, BELT sandwich, iced tea,
shortbread
Dinner–72 cents
Jambalaya, French bread, tea, ice box pudding
Total: $2.04

Day Three:
Breakfast–63 cents
Banana pancakes, Canadian bacon, coffee
Lunch–68 cents
Egg and avocado salad, quesadillas, iced tea
Dinner–63 cents
Chicken Kiev pop-ups, bric a broc, tea, shoo-fly pie
Total: $1.94

Day Four:
Breakfast–45 cents
Santa Fe Toast, 3 slices bacon, juice, coffee
Lunch–55 cents
Pizza, milk or lemonade, banana flambé

Dinner–88 cents
Ham croquettes, Lyonnaise potatoes, carrots and
leeks, tea, coconut mousse pie
Total: $1.88

Day Five:
Breakfast–42 cents
Fried apples & bacon, popovers, grits, coffee
Lunch–80 cents
Homemade beans & franks, oatmeal muffins, iced
tea, ice cream
Dinner–76 cents
Ravioli, grilled tomatoes, pepper rings, tea, shortcake
Total: $2.06

Day Six:
Breakfast–63 cents
Oatmeal, banana toast, coffee
Lunch–52 cents
Sloppy Joes, deviled eggs, iced tea, cookies
Dinner–86 cents
All American turkey with stuffing, fresh cranberry
sauce, carrot pie, blueberry squares, tea, apple pie
Total: $2.01

Day Seven:
Breakfast–32 cents
Poached eggs on toast, sausage, coffee
Lunch–74 cents
Cream of carrot soup, cheese sandwich, iced tea,
miracle cake
Dinner–89 cents
ABC Shortcut shortcake, corn on the cob, baked
onions, tea, chocolate mousse
Total: $1.87

For the seven days these menus cover, the average total spent each day per person is just a fraction under the magic number of $1.98. For the record, $1.98 is a whopping 46 percent less than the daily amount of food stamps given out by the government.

These seven menus do not exhaust the number of combinations that average out to only $1.98 a day. Not only is it possible to live on $1.98 a day, but it can be done in style and with variety. Nonetheless, being a cook, I know the value of a little fat here and there. So it is probably more reasonable to set a target of spending $2.50 to $2.75 a day on food costs–just about the average of all the menus in this book.

This means that the U.S. could cut food stamp costs by $1 a day and still provide more than is necessary to eat well–assuming the food stamp program also gave out a copy of this book!

But this is not a book for folks on food stamps. It is a book for any American who realizes he or she is spending too much on food costs.

How much could you save? I went back to the grocery store and priced the menus I presented in this chapter–but using commercially prepared products. The average cost per person per day soared to $6.05.

That's $4.10 more than you need to be spending. Each day. Or, to cast it in yearly terms, it is $1,500 more than anyone needs to spend each year.

If you have a family of four, it amounts to $6,000!

That is how much money you can save–$6,000 each year–if you follow the advice in this book. If you currently serve your family a lot of expensive pro-cessed foods, you can save a lot more–perhaps $10,000. That's enough to buy a new car!

And no one will ever suspect that you are "cutting corners"? Why would they? You are eating like a king!

Recipe Index

ABC   70
All-American Turkey   74
Almond Butter   151
Apple Pie   132
Appotatoes   31
Apricot Nut Bread   142
Asparagus soufflé   117
Avocado dressing   148

Bacorn Pie   113
Baked Atlanta   135
Baked Grapefruit   43
Baked Onions   119
Baked Stuffed Potato   106
Banana Bread   142
Banana dressing   148
Banana Nut Salad   51
Barbeque Sauce   150
Bearnaise sauce   150
Beef Brisket   75
Beef stock   46
Beef Stroganoff on Top   84
Biscuits   36, 42
Blue Cheese Dressing   148
Blueberry Squares   145
Boiled Potatoes   107
Breakfast Burritos   44
Bric-a-Broc   112
Brown Chow Stew   47
Bud Beef   80

3 C Salad   52
Cabbage in Cabbage   124
Cabbage Rolls   98
Canadian bacon   30
Cannelloni   83
Cantonese Stir Fry   90
Carrot Pie   123
Carrot soufflé   117
Carrots & Leeks   112
Catfish Curry   104
Caulimato Special   121
Chantilly Potatoes   107
Cheese Sauce   149
Chicken Fried Steak   97
Chicken Kiev Popups   72
Chicken stock   46
Chicken Veronica   104
Chili   58
Chili Sauce   58
Chinese Asparagus   111
Chocolate Mousse   127
Chocolate Waffles   129
Cocktail Sauce   150
Cocoa   152
Coconut Mousse Pie   133
Cole Slaw   53
Cookies   134

Corn Chowder   49
Corn on the Cob   113
Corn soufflé   117
Crab Louis   54
Cranberry Sauce   151
Cream of Carrot Soup   49
Creamed Chipped Beef   76
Creamed Onions   119
Creole Lima Beans   122
Crepes   32
Crescent Rolls   144
Curried Lima Bean Soup   47
Curry dressing   52

Daube   101
Deviled Eggs   68
Dill Sauce   149
Dinner Rolls   144
Dutch Family Cake   130
Dutch Kale   99

Egg and Avocado Salad   52
Eggs Benedict   44
English Muffins   143
Finnish Bread   141
Fish and Chips   89
Flour Tortillas   139
French dressing   148
French Peas   115
French Toast   35
Fried Apples & Bacon   37
Fried eggs   28
Fried Green Tomatoes   114
Fried Rice   67
Frontera Pork Chops   81

Great Zucchini!   120
Grilled Tomatoes   114
Grits   38
Guacamole   151

Ham and Asparagus On Top   86
Ham Croquettes   71
Hamburger Crunch   57
Hash   60
Hash browns   31
Hasty Pudding   39
Hollandaise Sauce   149
Homemade Beans & Franks   62
Honey Butter   151
Hot Fudge Sauce   129
Hot Sauce   150
Ice Box Pudding   136

Jambalaya   68

Lasagna   83
Lemon Soufflé   136

Lobster & Shrimp Soufflé   103
Lyonnaise Potatoes   107

MacCrab   63
Madeira Ham on Top   86
Majorcan Peas   115
Maltaise Sauce   150
Mashed potatoes   107
Meat Loaf of the Gods   77
Miracle Cake   128
Muffins   42
Mush   39
Mushroom Delight   43

Nassi Goreng   92
Nutmeg Snaps   123

1000 Island Dressing   148
O Sole Mio   94
Oatmeal   38
Oatmeal Raisin Cookie   134
Oatmeal Muffins   145
Omelets   56
Orange Juice   152

Paella   87
Pancakes   32
Pasta   146
Peeping Eggs   40
Pepper Rings   122
Perfect Popovers   34
Pie crust   131
Pita Bread   143
Pizza   61
Plum Good Salad   55
Poached eggs   29
Pork & Prunes   101
Pork Roast   89
Pot Roast   75
Potato Pancakes   109
Potato Salad   55
Potatoes Anna   108
Pumpkin Mush   39
Pumpkin Pie   131

Quesadillas   66

Ravioli   69
Rice Pilaf   111
Rouladen   95
Rye Bread   138

Salads   51
Sambal Oelek   92
Sandwiches   64
Sangría   152
Santa Fe Toast   35
Sateh Bami   100
Sausage   30, 41
Sausage biscuits   30
Scrambled eggs   28
Scrapple   39
Seafood Cream on Top   85

Serene Bread   139
Seven From Heaven   128
Shirred eggs   28—29
Shoo Fly Pie   133
Shortbread   130
Shortcake Supreme   127
Shrimp Bisque   50
Shrimp Curry   96
Shrimp Stir Fry   102
Slaw Dressing   149
Sloppy Joes   58
Sludge   91
Snert   48
Soft-boiled eggs   29
Soups   46
Sourdough French Bread   140
Spaghetti   82
Spaghetti Carbonara   82
Spinach Ham on Top   86
Spinach Soufflé   117
Steak and Lentils   97
Steak Fillups   59
Steamed Artichokes   120
Strata   41
Strawberry Shortcake   36
Sugar cookies   134
Surf & Turf on a Skewer   88
Surprises   134
Sweet Potato Puffs   110
Swiss Steak   76
Syrup   33
Szechuan Green Beans   116

T-Bone Bonus   100
Taco Salad   93
Tarragon Green Beans   116
Tartar Sauce   150
Toad in the Hole   40
Toast   42
Tomato Cream Sauce   149
Tomato Soup   48
Turkey Tetrazzini   93

Unfries   109

Vanilla Extract   151
Veal Francaise On Top   85
Veal Oscar Fillups   59
Veal Oscar Ravioli   69
Vegetable Stir Fry   118
Vegetable stock   46
Vichyssoise   50
Vinaigrette   148

Waffles   33
Waldorf Salad   54
White Bread   138
White Sauce   149

Yammies   110

Zucchini Spaghetti   82

160